MAKEUP
FOR BLACK WOMEN

TABLE OF CONTENTS

INTRODUCTION TO THE BOOK

COSPLAY IS MORE THAN JUST DRESSING UP—IT'S THE ART OF BRINGING CHARACTERS TO LIFE, TRANSFORMING YOURSELF INTO SOMEONE (OR SOMETHING) FROM ANOTHER WORLD, ANOTHER TIME, OR EVEN ANOTHER UNIVERSE. AT THE HEART OF THIS TRANSFORMATION IS MAKEUP, THE SECRET INGREDIENT THAT TAKES A COSTUME FROM GREAT TO EXTRAORDINARY. IT'S THE MAGIC TOUCH THAT ALLOWS YOU TO STEP INTO THE SHOES OF A FIERCE WARRIOR, A MISCHIEVOUS TRICKSTER, OR A HAUNTING PHANTOM.

IN THIS BOOK, YOU'LL FIND A WORLD OF POSSIBILITIES WHERE MAKEUP BECOMES YOUR MOST POWERFUL TOOL. FROM DRAMATIC, OTHERWORLDLY CREATIONS TO SUBTLE ENHANCEMENTS THAT BRING OUT A CHARACTER'S ESSENCE, THIS GUIDE IS FOR EVERYONE—FROM BEGINNERS TO EXPERIENCED MAKEUP ARTISTS LOOKING FOR NEW INSPIRATION. THE PROJECTS YOU'LL FIND HERE ARE DESIGNED TO SPARK YOUR CREATIVITY AND HELP YOU EXPLORE THE ENDLESS POTENTIAL OF COSPLAY MAKEUP.

EACH OF THE LOOKS WE'VE CRAFTED TELLS A STORY. THE BROKEN MASKED BEAUTY YOU SEE ON THE COVER, WITH HER ELEGANT YET SHATTERED FACADE, REPRESENTS A PERFECT FUSION OF BEAUTY AND MYSTERY—AN EMBODIMENT OF STRENGTH AND FRAGILITY, CAPTURED IN EVERY CAREFULLY PAINTED LINE. OTHER CHARACTERS WITHIN THESE PAGES CARRY THEIR OWN TALES: THE UNDEAD PIRATE CAPTAIN WITH HER WEATHERED, GHOSTLY FEATURES; THE GOTHIC VAMPIRE QUEEN WHOSE PIERCING GAZE AND PALE SKIN EVOKE A SENSE OF TIMELESS POWER; AND THE CIRCUS CLOWN, WHOSE EXAGGERATED, COLORFUL MAKEUP HIDES A DARKER, MORE CHAOTIC PERSONA BENEATH THE PLAYFUL EXTERIOR.

THESE LOOKS ARE MORE THAN JUST MAKEUP DESIGNS—THEY ARE PIECES OF ART, STORIES TOLD THROUGH COLOR, TEXTURE, AND FORM. AND NOW, IT'S YOUR TURN TO TELL THOSE STORIES IN YOUR OWN UNIQUE WAY.

WHY MAKEUP MATTERS IN COSPLAY

MAKEUP IS OFTEN OVERLOOKED IN COSPLAY, BUT IN TRUTH, IT CAN BE JUST AS IMPORTANT AS THE COSTUME ITSELF. IT HAS THE POWER TO CONVEY EMOTION, TRANSFORM A CHARACTER'S IDENTITY, AND SET THE TONE FOR THE ENTIRE COSPLAY. FOR EXAMPLE, THE SHARP LINES AND STARK COLORS OF A VILLAIN'S MAKEUP INSTANTLY COMMUNICATE DANGER AND INTRIGUE, WHILE THE SOFT, GLOWING HUES OF A MAGICAL HEROINE SUGGEST BEAUTY AND STRENGTH. WITH THE RIGHT MAKEUP, YOU CAN ELEVATE A CHARACTER, ADDING DEPTH AND DIMENSION THAT GOES FAR BEYOND WHAT A COSTUME CAN ACHIEVE ON ITS OWN.

COSPLAY MAKEUP IS ALSO ABOUT CREATING ILLUSIONS. IT'S ABOUT GIVING YOURSELF THE POWER TO STEP INTO SOMEONE ELSE'S SKIN FOR A DAY, WHETHER THAT SKIN IS SMOOTH, SCARRED, OR EVEN UNDEAD. THE MAKEUP TECHNIQUES IN THIS BOOK WILL HELP YOU CRAFT REALISTIC BATTLE WOUNDS, ACCENTUATE SHARP, REGAL FEATURES, OR EVEN MIMIC THE CRACKED PORCELAIN OF A DOLL'S FACE. WITH THE FLICK OF A BRUSH OR A CAREFULLY PLACED CONTOUR, YOU CAN CHANGE THE SHAPE OF YOUR NOSE, MAKE YOUR EYES APPEAR LARGER, OR GIVE YOURSELF OTHERWORLDLY TEXTURES THAT LOOK LIKE THEY'VE COME STRAIGHT FROM THE SCREEN OR PAGE.

UNLEASHING YOUR CREATIVITY

COSPLAY MAKEUP IS AN ART FORM WITHOUT LIMITS. WHETHER YOU'RE RECREATING AN ICONIC LOOK OR DESIGNING SOMETHING ENTIRELY NEW, THE POWER IS IN YOUR HANDS TO EXPRESS YOUR CREATIVITY. NO MATTER HOW AMBITIOUS OR SIMPLE THE CONCEPT, EVERY DESIGN IS AN OPPORTUNITY TO SHOW YOUR PERSONALITY, TO EXPERIMENT, AND TO PUSH THE

BOUNDARIES OF WHAT'S POSSIBLE WITH MAKEUP.

IN THIS BOOK, WE ENCOURAGE YOU TO PLAY. TRY NEW TECHNIQUES, MIX COLORS YOU WOULDN'T USUALLY PAIR, AND DON'T BE AFRAID TO MAKE MISTAKES. SOMETIMES, THE MOST UNEXPECTED COMBINATIONS CREATE THE MOST STRIKING RESULTS. YOU'LL LEARN EVERYTHING FROM PRECISION DETAILING—LIKE CREATING REALISTIC SCARS AND BRUISES—TO BOLD COLOR BLOCKING THAT BRINGS YOUR CHARACTERS' EMOTIONS TO THE FOREFRONT.

AND IT'S NOT JUST ABOUT HOW YOU LOOK—IT'S ABOUT HOW YOU FEEL. THE MOMENT YOU COMPLETE A MAKEUP LOOK AND CATCH YOUR REFLECTION IN THE MIRROR, YOU'RE NO LONGER YOURSELF. YOU'VE STEPPED INTO ANOTHER WORLD, EMBODYING A CHARACTER WHO EXISTS IN THAT SPACE BETWEEN REALITY AND FANTASY. THAT MOMENT OF TRANSFORMATION, WHEN YOU LOOK IN THE MIRROR AND SEE YOUR CREATION STARING BACK AT YOU, IS WHAT MAKES COSPLAY MAKEUP SO MAGICAL.

WHAT YOU'LL DISCOVER INSIDE

THIS BOOK IS FILLED WITH CAREFULLY CURATED DESIGNS, RANGING FROM DETAILED, INTRICATE CHARACTERS TO SIMPLER, POWERFUL LOOKS THAT CAN BE CREATED WITH MINIMAL PRODUCTS. YOU'LL LEARN HOW TO:

MASTER THE ART OF SHADING AND CONTOURING TO CHANGE THE SHAPE OF YOUR FACE

USE SPECIAL EFFECTS MAKEUP TO CREATE REALISTIC SCARS, WOUNDS, AND TEXTURES

APPLY BOLD COLORS AND CREATE STUNNING EYE DESIGNS THAT CAPTIVATE AND DRAW ATTENTION

COMBINE COSTUME ELEMENTS AND MAKEUP FOR A COHESIVE, CHARACTER-DRIVEN LOOK

WHETHER YOU'RE PREPARING FOR A CONVENTION, PHOTOSHOOT, OR JUST EXPLORING MAKEUP FOR THE FUN OF IT, THESE DESIGNS WILL OFFER YOU A WEALTH OF INSPIRATION AND GUIDANCE. EACH TUTORIAL IS BROKEN DOWN INTO EASY-TO-FOLLOW STEPS, ALLOWING YOU TO BUILD ON YOUR SKILLS AS YOU GO.

A WORLD OF POSSIBILITIES AWAITS

AT ITS CORE, COSPLAY MAKEUP IS ABOUT TRANSFORMATION, NOT JUST ON THE OUTSIDE, BUT ON THE INSIDE. WITH EVERY CHARACTER YOU EMBODY, YOU STEP INTO A DIFFERENT PERSONA. YOU BECOME A STORYTELLER, USING YOUR FACE AS THE CANVAS TO PAINT A TALE OF HEROISM, VILLAINY, MYSTERY, OR MAGIC.

THIS BOOK ISN'T JUST ABOUT TEACHING TECHNIQUES—IT'S ABOUT UNLOCKING YOUR POTENTIAL AS AN ARTIST AND A COSPLAYER. EACH LOOK, EACH TUTORIAL, IS A GATEWAY TO ENDLESS POSSIBILITIES, AND WE HOPE THAT THROUGH THESE PAGES, YOU'LL DISCOVER NEW WAYS TO EXPRESS YOURSELF AND BRING YOUR FAVORITE CHARACTERS TO LIFE.

SO, WHETHER YOU'RE HERE TO CREATE A LOOK THAT'S FIERCE, FUN, DARK, OR DELIGHTFUL, WE INVITE YOU TO EXPLORE, EXPERIMENT, AND, MOST IMPORTANTLY, ENJOY THE PROCESS. AFTER ALL, THE TRUE MAGIC OF COSPLAY MAKEUP LIES IN THE JOURNEY AS MUCH AS IN THE FINAL TRANSFORMATION.

WELCOME TO THE WORLD OF COSPLAY MAKEUP. LET YOUR CREATIVITY SOAR, AND LET THE TRANSFORMATIONS BEGIN!

HEALTH AND SAFETY GUIDELINES FOR MAKEUP APPLICATION

CLEAN HANDS:

ALWAYS WASH YOUR HANDS BEFORE AND AFTER APPLYING MAKEUP. CLEAN HANDS PREVENT THE TRANSFER OF BACTERIA TO YOUR SKIN AND MAKEUP PRODUCTS, MINIMIZING THE RISK OF INFECTIONS.

TOOL HYGIENE:

ENSURE THAT ALL MAKEUP TOOLS, SUCH AS BRUSHES, SPONGES, AND APPLICATORS, ARE CLEAN BEFORE USE. REGULARLY WASH YOUR BRUSHES AND REPLACE SPONGES TO AVOID THE BUILDUP OF BACTERIA AND COSMETIC RESIDUE.

PRODUCT TESTING:

BEFORE APPLYING NEW COSMETICS TO YOUR FACE, CONDUCT AN ALLERGY TEST. APPLY A SMALL AMOUNT OF THE PRODUCT ON THE INSIDE OF YOUR WRIST OR BEHIND YOUR EAR AND WAIT 24 HOURS TO ENSURE IT DOESN'T CAUSE AN ALLERGIC REACTION.

AVOID CONTACT WITH EYES:

WHEN APPLYING COSMETICS AROUND THE EYES, BE ESPECIALLY CAREFUL. AVOID GETTING MAKEUP INTO YOUR EYES TO PREVENT IRRITATION OR DAMAGE.

SAFE STORAGE OF COSMETICS:

STORE COSMETICS IN A COOL, DRY PLACE AWAY FROM DIRECT SUNLIGHT. ENSURE THEY ARE TIGHTLY SEALED TO AVOID CONTAMINATION AND EXTEND THEIR SHELF LIFE.

EXPIRATION DATES:

PAY ATTENTION TO THE EXPIRATION DATES OF COSMETICS. DO NOT USE PRODUCTS BEYOND THEIR EXPIRATION DATE, AS THEY MAY LOSE THEIR EFFECTIVENESS OR BECOME UNSAFE FOR YOUR SKIN.

SKIN REST:

AFTER THE EVENT OR PHOTO SESSION, REMEMBER TO THOROUGHLY CLEANSE YOUR FACE OF ALL MAKEUP PRODUCTS. ALLOW YOUR SKIN TO BREATHE AND REJUVENATE BY APPLYING A MOISTURIZING CREAM.

AVOID SHARING COSMETICS:

MAKEUP PRODUCTS SUCH AS LIPSTICKS, MASCARAS, AND FOUNDATIONS ARE MEANT FOR PERSONAL USE. SHARING THEM CAN LEAD TO THE SPREAD OF BACTERIA AND VIRUSES.

USE SAFE PRODUCTS:

MAKE SURE ALL THE COSMETICS YOU USE ARE SAFE FOR SKIN APPLICATION AND HAVE THE APPROPRIATE SAFETY CERTIFICATIONS. AVOID PRODUCTS CONTAINING INGREDIENTS TO WHICH YOU ARE ALLERGIC.

FOLLOWING THESE HEALTH AND SAFETY GUIDELINES WILL HELP YOU ENJOY CREATING MAKEUP LOOKS IN A SAFE AND HYGIENIC MANNER, ENSURING THE BEST RESULTS WITHOUT COMPROMISING YOUR HEALTH. CREATE, EXPERIMENT, AND HAVE FUN, ALL WHILE STAYING SAFE!

VIBRANT REBEL COSPLAY: HEARTS AND COLORS

STEP-BY-STEP INSTRUCTIONS:

SKIN PREPARATION:

START WITH CLEAN, MOISTURIZED SKIN. APPLY A PRIMER TO SMOOTH THE SKIN AND HELP THE MAKEUP LAST. FOLLOW UP WITH A FOUNDATION THAT MATCHES YOUR SKIN TONE FOR EVEN COVERAGE.

EYESHADOW AND EYELINER:

APPLY RED EYESHADOW TO ONE EYELID AND BLUE TO THE OTHER, BLENDING SMOOTHLY. USE BLACK EYELINER TO CREATE A SHARP LINE ALONG THE UPPER LASH LINE, ADDING A WING FOR A DRAMATIC TOUCH.

HEARTS AND WHITE MARKINGS:

USE RED AND BLUE LIQUID EYELINER OR FACE PAINT TO DRAW HEART SHAPES ON YOUR FOREHEAD AND CHEEKS. APPLY WHITE FACE PAINT TO DRAW SYMMETRICAL TRIANGLES UNDER EACH EYE FOR ADDED CONTRAST.

BROWS AND LASHES:

DEFINE YOUR BROWS WITH A DARK PENCIL FOR A NEAT, SHARP SHAPE. APPLY MASCARA OR FALSE LASHES FOR A FULLER, MORE INTENSE LOOK.

LIPS:

APPLY A BOLD RED LIPSTICK WITH A MATTE FINISH TO COMPLETE THE VIBRANT LOOK. USE A LIP LINER FOR PRECISE DEFINITION AND TO KEEP THE LIPSTICK IN PLACE.

FINAL TOUCHES:

STYLE YOUR HAIR IN TWO PONYTAILS WITH RED AND BLUE COLORS. ADD A BLACK CHOKER FOR A REBELLIOUS VIBE AND SET YOUR MAKEUP WITH A SETTING SPRAY TO ENSURE IT LASTS THROUGHOUT THE DAY OR EVENT.

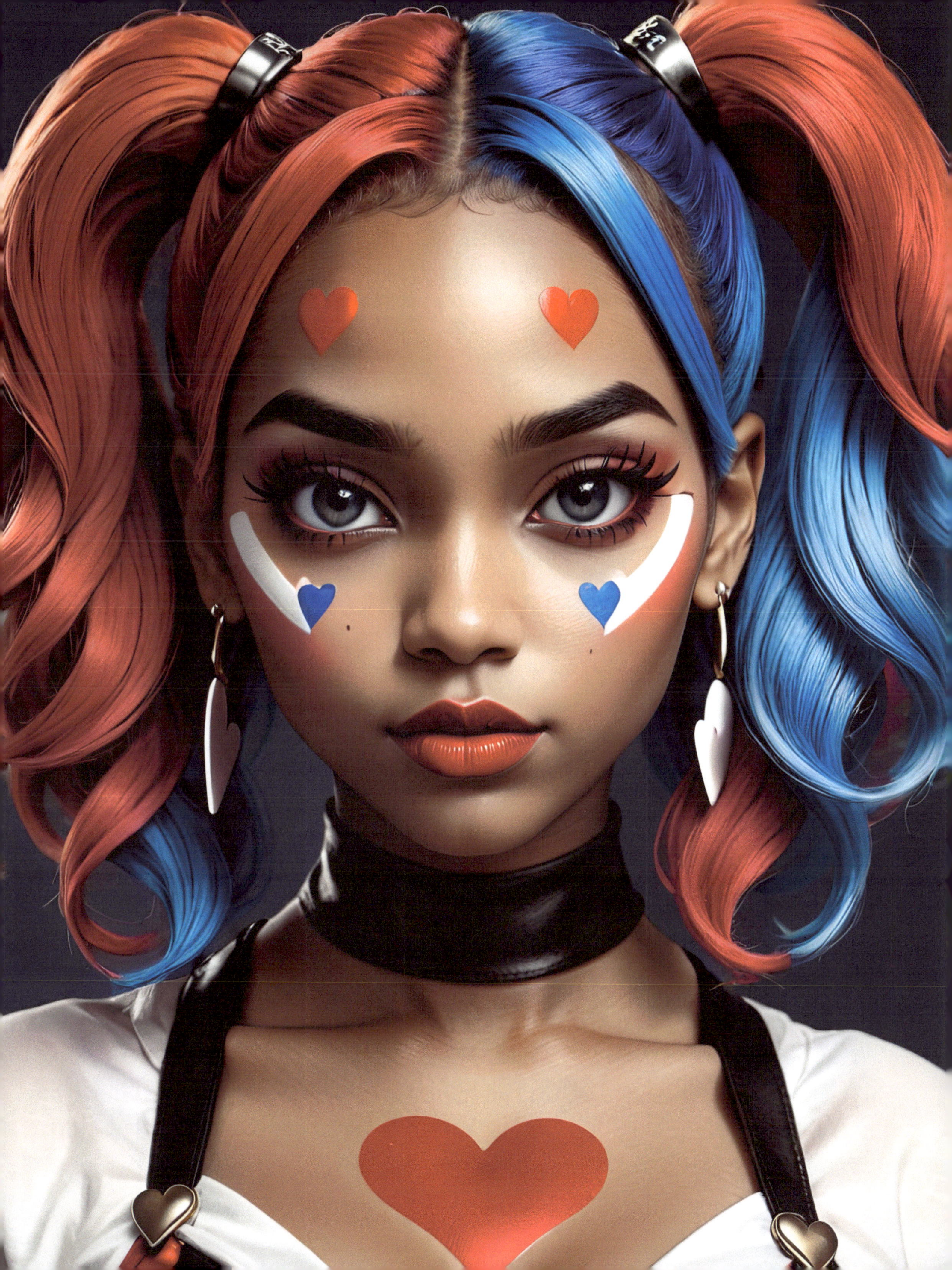

NIGHTMARE CLAW COSPLAY MAKEUP

STEP-BY-STEP INSTRUCTIONS:

SKIN PREPARATION:

CLEANSE AND MOISTURIZE YOUR SKIN THOROUGHLY. APPLY A PRIMER FOR SMOOTH APPLICATION, FOLLOWED BY A FOUNDATION THAT MATCHES YOUR SKIN TONE. LIGHTLY CONTOUR YOUR CHEEKBONES, JAWLINE, AND TEMPLES TO DEFINE YOUR FACE.

EYESHADOW AND EYELINER:

USE BLACK AND BURGUNDY EYESHADOWS, BLENDING THE BLACK ON THE OUTER CORNERS AND THE BURGUNDY NEAR THE LASH LINE. APPLY BLACK EYELINER ALONG THE UPPER LASH LINE, CREATING A SMALL WING FOR ADDED DRAMA.

CLAW MARKS:

WITH A FINE BRUSH, PAINT JAGGED RED CLAW MARKS ON YOUR CHEEKS AND FOREHEAD. ADD DARKER RED OR BURGUNDY AROUND THE EDGES FOR A REALISTIC, BLOOD-LIKE EFFECT, MIMICKING FRESH SCRATCHES.

BROWS AND LASHES:

SHAPE YOUR BROWS WITH A DARK PENCIL, KEEPING THEM SHARP AND DEFINED. APPLY A FEW COATS OF VOLUMIZING MASCARA OR OPT FOR FALSE LASHES TO ENHANCE THE EYES.

LIPS:

KEEP THE LIPS NEUTRAL WITH A DEEP BROWN OR DARK NUDE LIPSTICK, PREFERABLY WITH A MATTE FINISH TO COMPLEMENT THE GOTHIC AESTHETIC.

FINAL TOUCHES:

STYLE YOUR HAIR WITH SOFT WAVES FOR ADDED TEXTURE. COMPLETE THE LOOK WITH A BLACK CHOKER, AND SET YOUR MAKEUP WITH A SETTING SPRAY FOR LONG-LASTING WEAR.

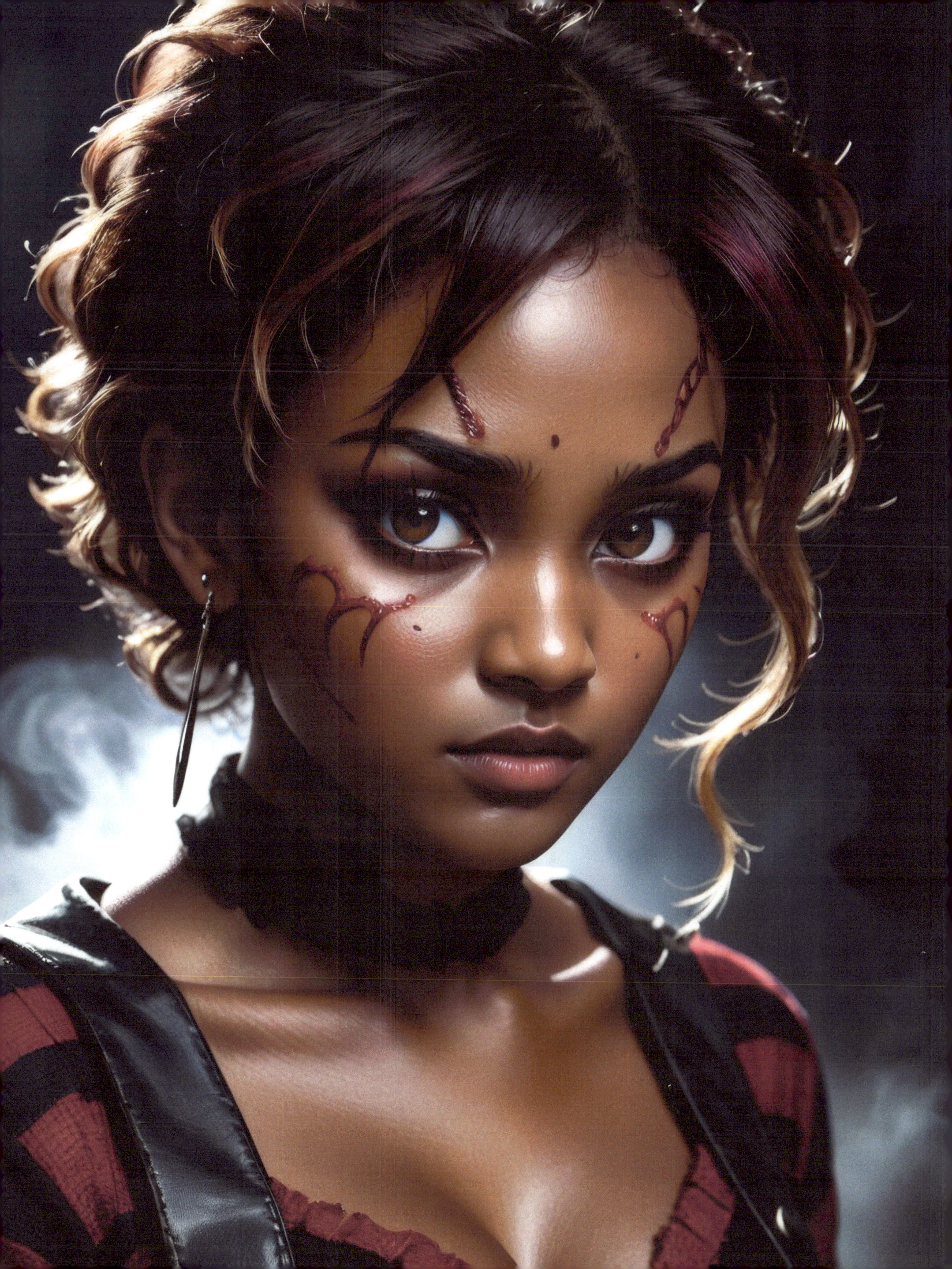

FIERY DEMON COSPLAY MAKEUP

STEP-BY-STEP INSTRUCTIONS:

SKIN PREPARATION:

CLEANSE AND MOISTURIZE YOUR SKIN TO ENSURE A SMOOTH APPLICATION. USE A PRIMER TO CREATE A PERFECT BASE FOR THE MAKEUP. APPLY A MEDIUM-COVERAGE FOUNDATION THAT MATCHES YOUR SKIN TONE TO EVEN OUT THE COMPLEXION.

FACE DESIGN:

USE BLACK AND RED FACE PAINT TO CREATE THE INTRICATE GEOMETRIC PATTERNS SEEN ON THE FOREHEAD AND CHEEKS. START WITH THE BLACK LINES, SHAPING THEM AROUND THE FOREHEAD AND EYES, THEN FILL IN THE GAPS WITH RED. USE A FINE BRUSH FOR PRECISION.

EYESHADOW AND EYELINER:

APPLY A SUBTLE NEUTRAL EYESHADOW TO LET THE FACE DESIGN STAND OUT. USE BLACK EYELINER TO DEFINE YOUR UPPER LASH LINE, EXTENDING IT INTO A SOFT WING TO COMPLEMENT THE SHARP LINES OF THE FACE PAINT.

BROWS AND LASHES:

DEFINE THE BROWS USING A DARK BROW PENCIL, SHAPING THEM NATURALLY BUT SHARPLY TO ALIGN WITH THE FIERCE LOOK. APPLY MASCARA OR FALSE LASHES TO ENHANCE THE EYES, MAKING THEM MORE DRAMATIC AGAINST THE BOLD FACE DESIGN.

LIPS:

APPLY A DEEP RED MATTE LIPSTICK TO BALANCE THE RED AND BLACK DESIGN ON THE FACE. ENSURE CLEAN LINES BY USING A LIP LINER IN A SIMILAR SHADE FOR PRECISION.

FINAL TOUCHES:

STYLE YOUR HAIR INTO SLEEK, PULLED-BACK BUNS OR ATTACH PROSTHETIC HORNS FOR AN EXTRA DEMON-LIKE APPEARANCE. SET THE ENTIRE LOOK WITH A MAKEUP SETTING SPRAY TO ENSURE IT LASTS FOR COSPLAY EVENTS OR PARTIES.

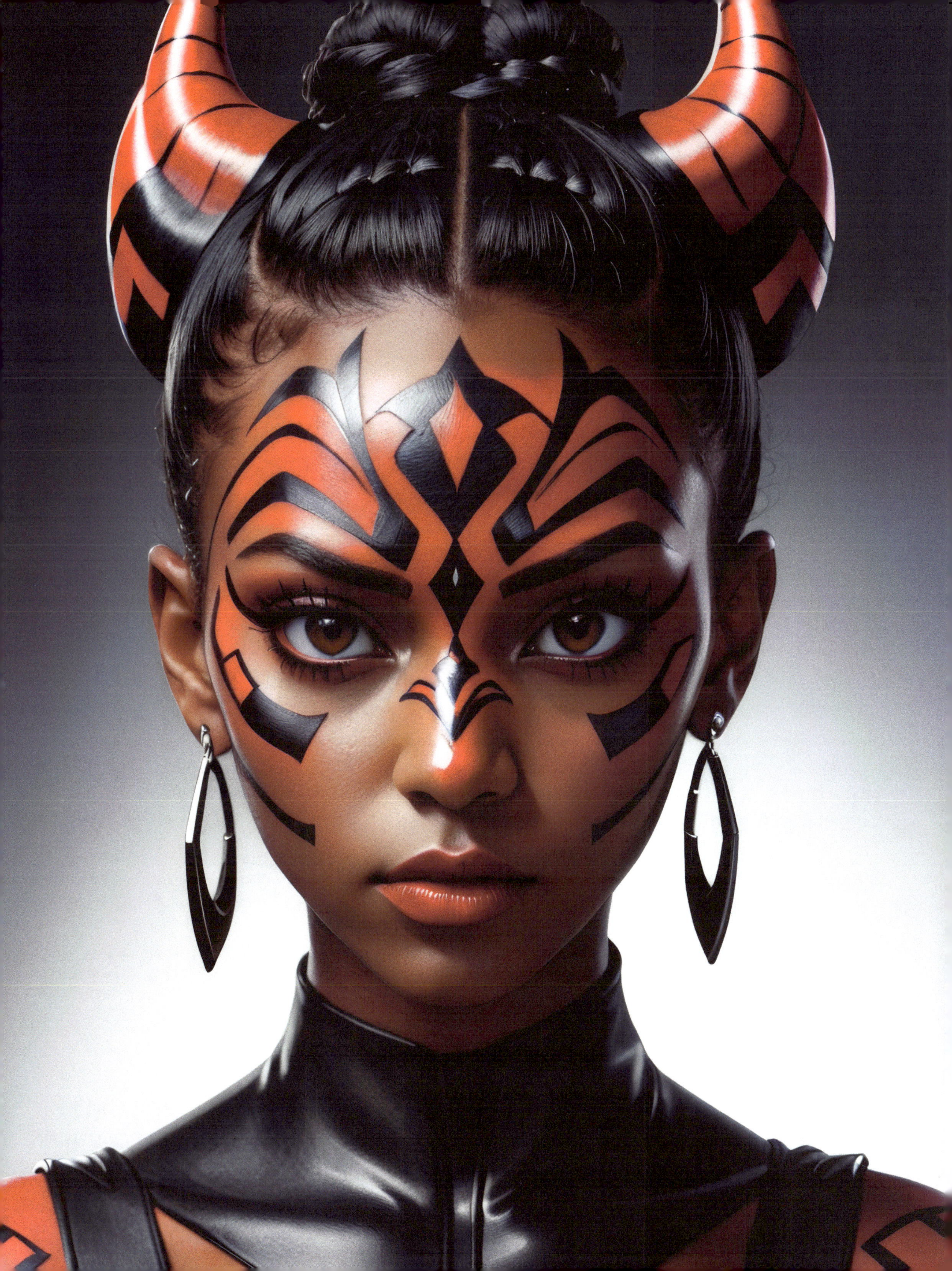

FROST QUEEN COSPLAY MAKEUP

STEP-BY-STEP INSTRUCTIONS:

SKIN PREPARATION:

START BY CLEANSING AND MOISTURIZING YOUR SKIN. APPLY A PRIMER FOR A SMOOTH BASE, FOLLOWED BY A MEDIUM-COVERAGE FOUNDATION THAT MATCHES YOUR SKIN TONE TO CREATE AN EVEN COMPLEXION.

FACE DESIGN:

USE WHITE AND BLACK FACE PAINT TO CREATE THE BOLD, ICY SHAPES AROUND THE FOREHEAD AND EYES. BEGIN BY OUTLINING THE DESIGN WITH BLACK, THEN FILL IN THE SPACES WITH WHITE FOR CONTRAST. USE A FINE BRUSH FOR THE DETAILED LINES, ESPECIALLY AROUND THE FOREHEAD JEWEL.

EYESHADOW AND EYELINER:

APPLY COOL-TONED BLUE EYESHADOW ACROSS THE LIDS, BLENDING OUTWARD INTO A SOFT GRADIENT. LINE YOUR UPPER LASH LINE WITH BLACK EYELINER, CREATING A WINGED EFFECT THAT COMPLEMENTS THE SHARP EDGES OF THE FACE PAINT.

BROWS AND LASHES:

DEFINE THE BROWS NATURALLY USING A LIGHT OR MEDIUM BROWN BROW PENCIL TO BALANCE THE COOL-TONED MAKEUP. APPLY FALSE LASHES OR VOLUMIZING MASCARA TO MAKE YOUR EYES POP AGAINST THE FROSTY FACE DESIGN.

LIPS:

USE A DEEP PURPLE MATTE LIPSTICK TO COMPLETE THE FROSTY QUEEN AESTHETIC. LINE THE LIPS WITH A SIMILAR-COLORED LIP LINER FOR CLEAN, SHARP EDGES.

FINAL TOUCHES:

STYLE YOUR HAIR IN AN ICY, SPIKED FASHION OR WEAR A PLATINUM WIG WITH VOLUME. ACCESSORIZE WITH BLUE GEMSTONES OR JEWELS, AS SEEN IN THE DESIGN. SET EVERYTHING WITH A MAKEUP SETTING SPRAY FOR LONG-LASTING WEAR.

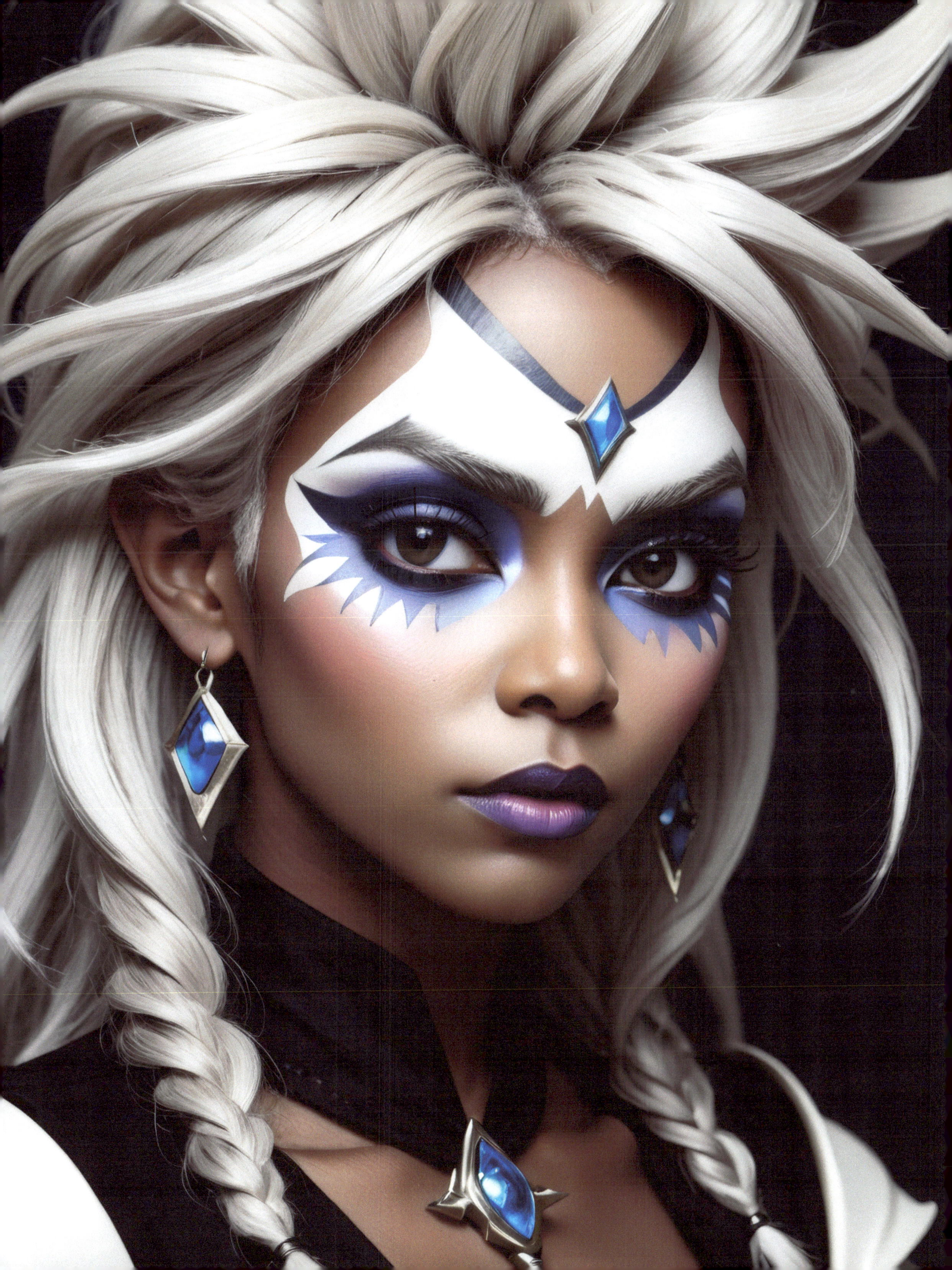

PHANTOM PRIESTESS COSPLAY MAKEUP

STEP-BY-STEP INSTRUCTIONS:

SKIN PREPARATION:

CLEANSE AND MOISTURIZE YOUR SKIN THOROUGHLY. APPLY A PRIMER TO SMOOTH THE SKIN AND CREATE AN EVEN BASE. USE A LIGHT TO MEDIUM COVERAGE FOUNDATION TO EVEN OUT YOUR COMPLEXION, FOCUSING ON AREAS NOT COVERED BY THE FACE PAINT.

WHITE BASE PAINT:

COVER THE ENTIRE FACE WITH A WHITE, MATTE FACE PAINT. USE A SPONGE OR BRUSH FOR AN EVEN APPLICATION, MAKING SURE TO COVER ALL VISIBLE AREAS, ESPECIALLY AROUND THE EYES AND MOUTH.

BLACK FACE DETAILING:

USING BLACK FACE PAINT, CREATE DRAMATIC, CURVED LINES EXTENDING FROM THE EYES AND MOUTH. CAREFULLY DRAW THE SHARP, SYMMETRICAL LINES THAT FRAME THE EYES AND TRAIL DOWN THE FACE, GIVING IT A HAUNTING AND MYSTERIOUS APPEARANCE.

EYES AND LASHES:

APPLY BLACK EYESHADOW TO DEEPEN THE AREA AROUND THE EYES. USE BLACK EYELINER TO CREATE SHARP DEFINITION, FOLLOWING THE NATURAL CURVE OF THE FACE PAINT DESIGN. ADD VOLUMINOUS BLACK MASCARA OR FALSE LASHES FOR A BOLD FINISH.

LIPS:

PAINT THE LIPS WITH BLACK LIPSTICK, AND EXTEND THE DESIGN DOWNWARD WITH A VERTICAL BLACK LINE FROM THE LOWER LIP TO THE CHIN. MAKE SURE THE LINES ARE CLEAN AND SYMMETRICAL FOR A POLISHED LOOK.

FINAL TOUCHES:

STYLE THE HAIR IN A SLEEK, PULLED-BACK MANNER OR WEAR A DARK HOOD AS SEEN IN THE IMAGE. ACCESSORIZE WITH GOLD EARRINGS FOR A CONTRASTING EFFECT, AND SET THE ENTIRE LOOK WITH SETTING SPRAY FOR LONG-LASTING WEAR.

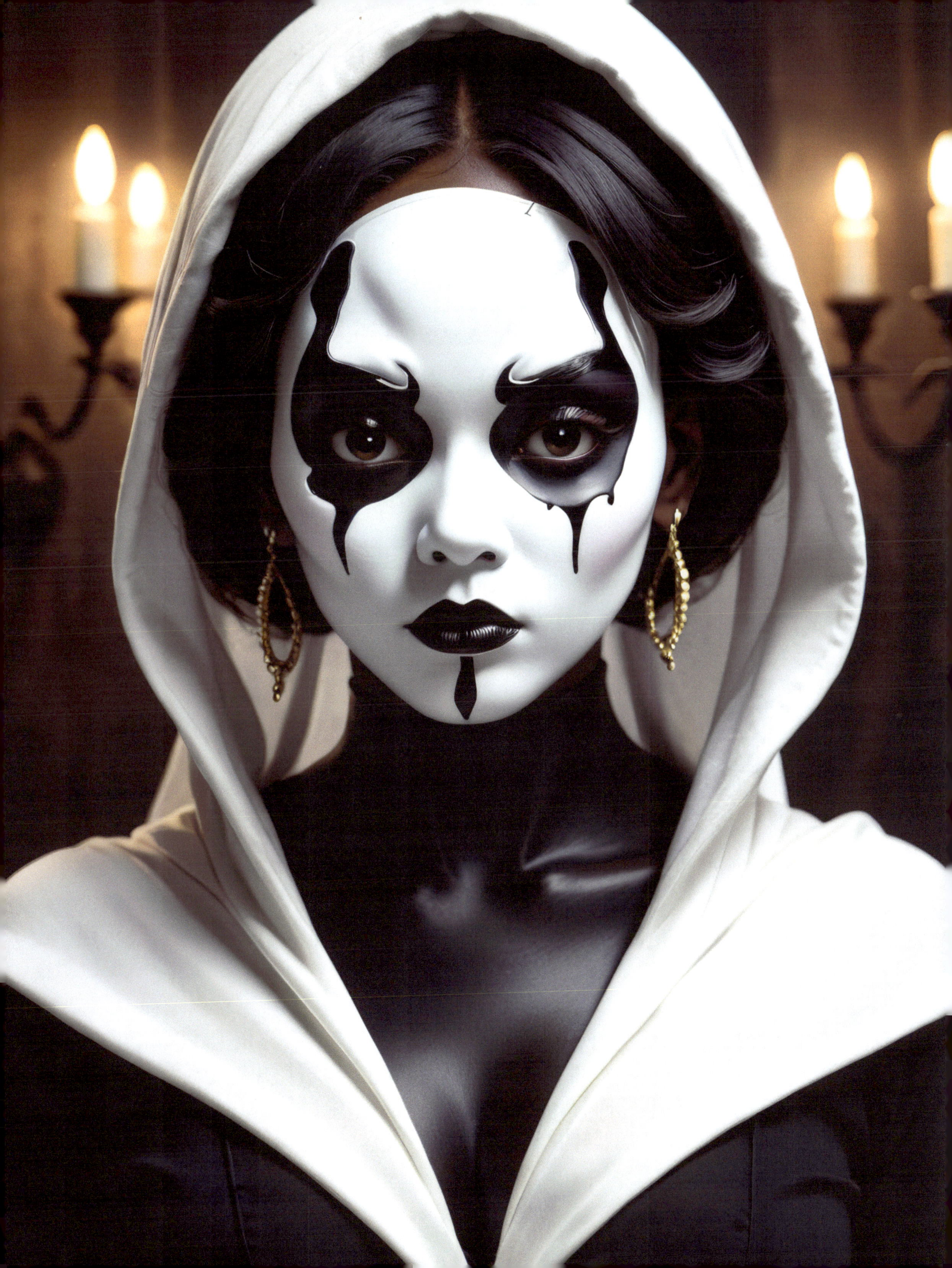

HELLBOUND WARRIOR COSPLAY MAKEUP

STEP-BY-STEP INSTRUCTIONS:

SKIN PREPARATION:

CLEANSE AND MOISTURIZE YOUR SKIN TO ENSURE A SMOOTH BASE. APPLY A PRIMER TO PROLONG THE MAKEUP WEAR, FOLLOWED BY A MEDIUM-COVERAGE FOUNDATION THAT MATCHES YOUR SKIN TONE FOR A FLAWLESS FINISH.

EYEBROWS AND CONTOURING:

SHAPE YOUR EYEBROWS WITH A BROW PENCIL FOR A SHARP AND DEFINED LOOK. LIGHTLY CONTOUR YOUR CHEEKBONES, TEMPLES, AND JAWLINE TO CREATE A STRONG, SCULPTED APPEARANCE.

EYESHADOW AND EYELINER:

APPLY A NEUTRAL-TONED EYESHADOW TO KEEP THE EYES SUBTLE, ALLOWING THE OVERALL LOOK TO STAND OUT. USE BLACK EYELINER TO LINE YOUR UPPER LASH LINE, AND ADD TINY DECORATIVE BLACK DOTS OR METAL STUDS AROUND THE EYES FOR A HELLRAISER-INSPIRED TOUCH.

LASHES AND MASCARA:

CURL YOUR LASHES AND APPLY VOLUMIZING MASCARA. FOR A BOLDER LOOK, CONSIDER NATURAL-LOOKING FALSE LASHES TO ENHANCE THE EYES WITHOUT OVERPOWERING THE FACIAL DETAILS.

FACE STUDS AND HIGHLIGHTER:

APPLY SMALL METALLIC STUDS OR ADHESIVE RHINESTONES IN A SYMMETRICAL LINE DOWN THE CENTER OF YOUR FOREHEAD AND NOSE, MIMICKING A PINHEAD-INSPIRED AESTHETIC. USE HIGHLIGHTER ON THE CHEEKBONES, BROW BONE, AND NOSE BRIDGE FOR AN ETHEREAL GLOW.

FINAL TOUCHES:

STYLE YOUR HAIR WITH PLATINUM-WHITE BRAIDS OR TEXTURED LOCKS, INCORPORATING METALLIC SPIKES OR STUDS TO REFLECT THE HELLRAISER THEME. ADD A STATEMENT CHOKER AND MATCHING ARMOR-LIKE ACCESSORIES TO COMPLETE THE LOOK. FINISH WITH A SETTING SPRAY TO LOCK IN THE MAKEUP FOR LONG-LASTING WEAR.

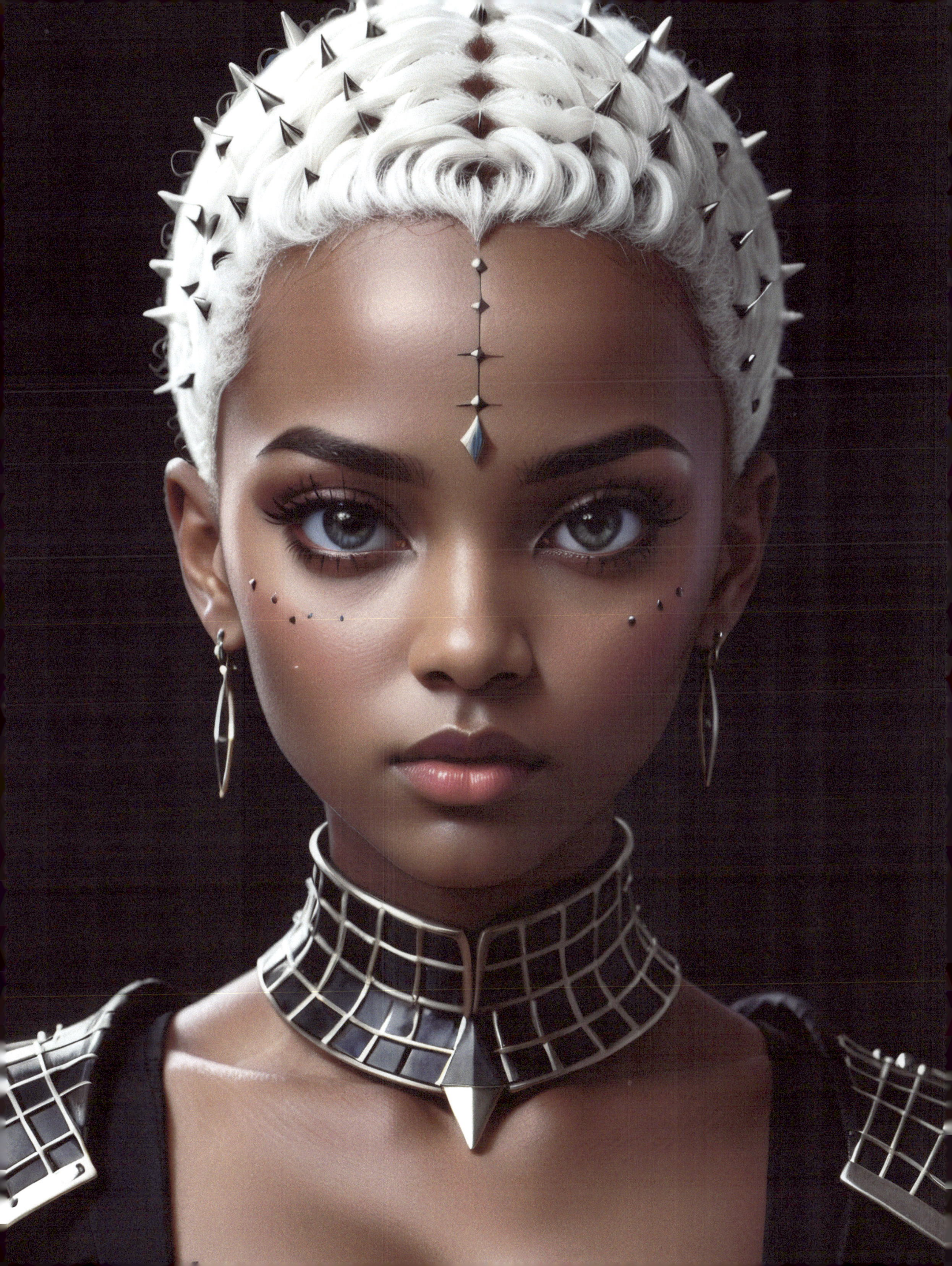

CHAOTIC JESTER COSPLAY MAKEUP

STEP-BY-STEP INSTRUCTIONS:

SKIN PREPARATION:

START WITH CLEAN AND MOISTURIZED SKIN. APPLY A PRIMER FOR SMOOTHNESS AND LONG-LASTING WEAR, FOLLOWED BY A FULL-COVERAGE FOUNDATION. FOCUS ON AREAS NOT COVERED BY THE WHITE FACE PAINT.

WHITE BASE PAINT:

COVER THE ENTIRE FACE WITH WHITE FACE PAINT, USING A SPONGE OR BRUSH FOR AN EVEN, OPAQUE FINISH. BLEND IT WELL INTO THE HAIRLINE AND DOWN TO THE JAWLINE FOR A SEAMLESS EFFECT.

EYESHADOW AND DARK CIRCLES:

APPLY BLACK OR DARK PURPLE EYESHADOW AROUND THE EYES, EXTENDING OUTWARD IN A MESSY, CHAOTIC FASHION. ADD BLACK EYELINER TO DEFINE THE EYES AND GIVE THEM A SHARP, INTENSE LOOK. SMUDGE THE EDGES FOR A ROUGH, WORN EFFECT.

SMUDGED RED LIPS AND FACE LINES:

PAINT THE LIPS WITH A DEEP RED LIPSTICK. EXTEND THE COLOR OUTWARD, CREATING EXAGGERATED, SMUDGED LINES ON BOTH SIDES OF THE MOUTH FOR A SINISTER GRIN. ADD FAINT RED LINES AROUND THE FOREHEAD TO MIMIC WRINKLES AND AN UNKEMPT LOOK.

BROWS AND FOREHEAD CREASES:

USE DARK BROWN OR BLACK EYESHADOW TO DEFINE THE BROWS, GIVING THEM AN ARCHED, EXPRESSIVE SHAPE. LIGHTLY DRAW IN FOREHEAD CREASES WITH BLACK OR BROWN EYELINER TO EMPHASIZE A MENACING EXPRESSION.

FINAL TOUCHES:

STYLE THE HAIR IN MESSY, TOUSLED WAVES, WITH GREEN COLORING ADDED FOR A BOLD FINISH. WEAR A PURPLE COAT OR COSTUME TO COMPLETE THE JESTER-INSPIRED LOOK, AND USE SETTING SPRAY TO KEEP THE MAKEUP IN PLACE THROUGHOUT THE EVENT.

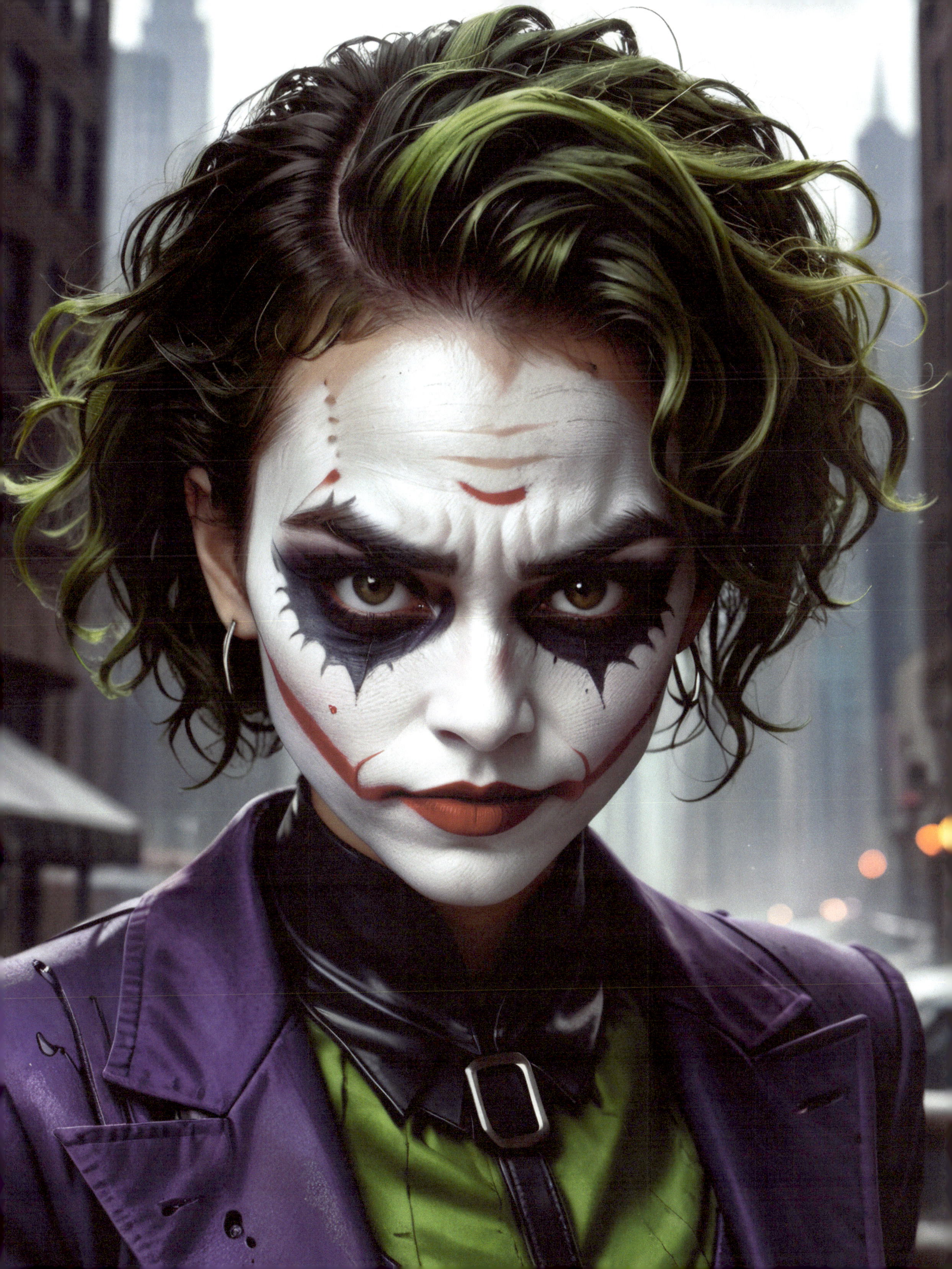

CARNIVAL CHAOS COSPLAY MAKEUP

STEP-BY-STEP INSTRUCTIONS:

SKIN PREPARATION:

Cleanse and moisturize your face to ensure smooth makeup application. Apply a primer to help the makeup last longer, followed by a medium-coverage foundation, focusing on areas that won't be covered by the white face paint.

WHITE BASE PAINT:

Cover your entire face with white face paint using a makeup sponge or brush for an even, opaque finish. Make sure to blend the edges into your hairline and down to your neck for a seamless look.

EYESHADOW AND EYELINER:

Apply vibrant blue eyeshadow to the lids, blending it into the crease. Use black eyeliner to create sharp, winged lines on both upper and lower lash lines, enhancing the dramatic clown-inspired look. Add false lashes for extra flair.

RED AND BLACK FACE DETAILS:

Using red face paint, create heart-like shapes above the eyebrows and extend red lines from the corners of your mouth. Outline the lips with red lipstick, adding a sharp point extending below the bottom lip. Add small black dots near the eyes for extra detailing.

LIPS:

Apply a bright red lipstick to the lips, ensuring crisp lines with a lip liner for precision. The lips should have a classic clownish curve, but still look refined and sharp.

FINAL TOUCHES:

Style your hair in voluminous curls with a vibrant mix of purple and pink, enhancing the carnival theme. Set the entire look with setting spray for long-lasting wear, and pair it with a colorful, carnival-themed outfit to complete the look.

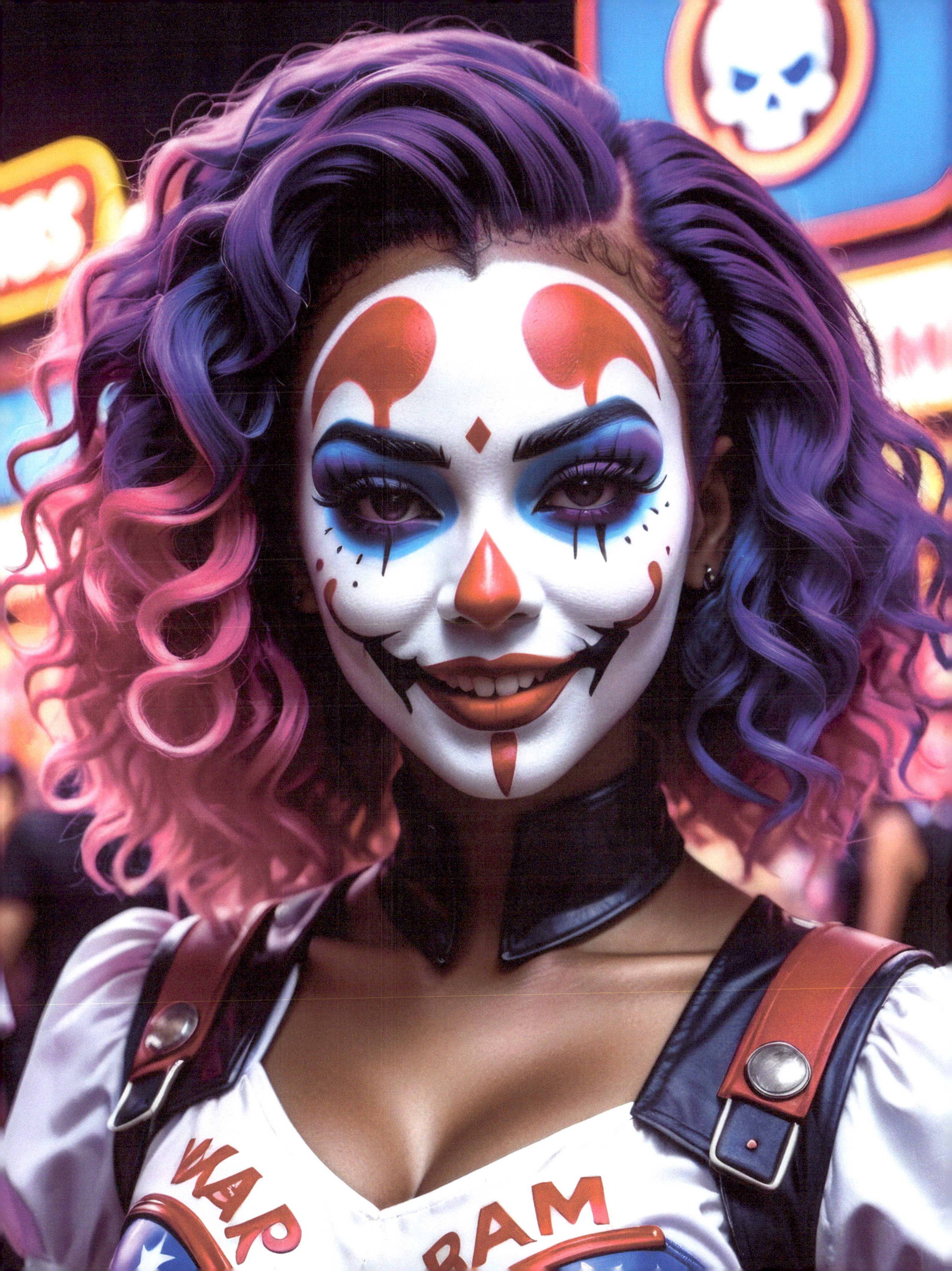

WAR
BAM

PLAYFUL PERFORMER COSPLAY MAKEUP

STEP-BY-STEP INSTRUCTIONS:

SKIN PREPARATION:

CLEANSE AND MOISTURIZE YOUR FACE TO PREP FOR MAKEUP. APPLY A PRIMER TO HELP THE MAKEUP LAST LONGER, FOLLOWED BY A FOUNDATION THAT MATCHES YOUR SKIN TONE FOR AN EVEN BASE.

EYESHADOW AND BROWS:

APPLY VIBRANT PURPLE EYESHADOW ON THE EYELIDS, BLENDING IT OUTWARDS FOR A BOLD, STRIKING LOOK. SHAPE AND DEFINE THE BROWS USING A DARK BROW PENCIL, KEEPING THEM SHARP AND WELL-GROOMED TO COMPLEMENT THE BRIGHT EYESHADOW.

FACE DETAILING:

USING WHITE FACE PAINT, CREATE SMALL OVAL SHAPES ON BOTH CHEEKS. INSIDE THE OVALS, PAINT SMALL RED AND BLUE HEARTS OR CIRCLES TO ADD A PLAYFUL TOUCH.

EYELINER AND LASHES:

LINE YOUR UPPER LASH LINE WITH BLACK EYELINER, EXTENDING IT SLIGHTLY FOR A WINGED EFFECT. APPLY VOLUMINOUS FALSE LASHES OR SEVERAL COATS OF MASCARA TO ENHANCE THE EYES AND ADD DRAMA.

LIPS: USE A BOLD, MATTE RED LIPSTICK TO DEFINE THE LIPS, ENSURING CLEAN AND PRECISE LINES. CONSIDER USING A LIP LINER TO HELP SHAPE THE LIPS AND KEEP THE COLOR INTACT.

FINAL TOUCHES:

STYLE YOUR HAIR INTO TWO PLAYFUL PIGTAILS WITH VOLUMINOUS CURLS. ADD VIBRANT PURPLE AND PINK EXTENSIONS OR TEMPORARY HAIR COLOR TO MATCH THE MAKEUP. FINISH THE LOOK WITH A SETTING SPRAY TO KEEP THE MAKEUP IN PLACE, AND PAIR WITH A COLORFUL, PERFORMANCE-INSPIRED OUTFIT FOR A COMPLETE TRANSFORMATION.

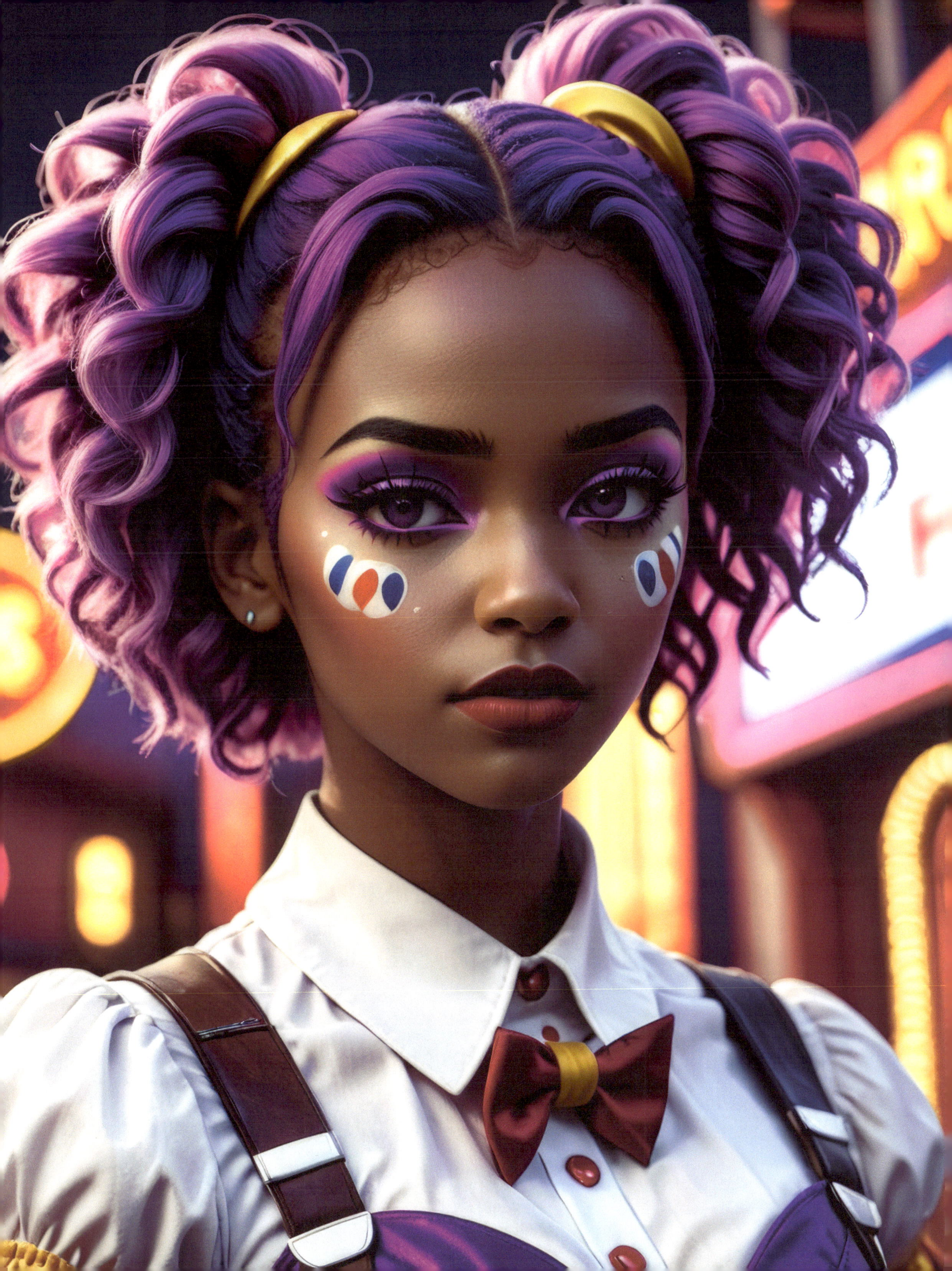

SKELETON SIREN COSPLAY MAKEUP

STEP-BY-STEP INSTRUCTIONS:

SKIN PREPARATION:

CLEANSE AND MOISTURIZE YOUR FACE TO ENSURE SMOOTH MAKEUP APPLICATION. APPLY A PRIMER TO CREATE A LONG-LASTING BASE. USE A FOUNDATION THAT MATCHES YOUR SKIN TONE ON AREAS NOT COVERED BY THE WHITE FACE PAINT.

WHITE SKULL BASE:

APPLY WHITE FACE PAINT EVENLY OVER THE FACE, FOCUSING ON CREATING A SHARP, SKULL-LIKE STRUCTURE AROUND THE EYES AND CHEEKS. USE A BRUSH OR SPONGE FOR SMOOTH APPLICATION, BLENDING CAREFULLY AROUND THE HAIRLINE AND NECK.

EYESHADOW AND HOLLOW EYES:

APPLY DEEP PURPLE EYESHADOW AROUND THE EYES IN A CIRCULAR SHAPE, EXTENDING IT OUTWARDS FOR A HOLLOW, SUNKEN LOOK. USE BLACK FACE PAINT TO DRAW JAGGED LINES AROUND THE EYE SOCKETS, GIVING THE ILLUSION OF STITCHED EYELIDS.

NOSE AND MOUTH:

USE BLACK FACE PAINT TO CREATE THE TRIANGULAR SKELETON NOSE. FOR THE MOUTH, DRAW THIN BLACK LINES EXTENDING FROM THE LIPS TO THE SIDES OF THE CHEEKS, MIMICKING SKELETAL TEETH. ADD SHORT VERTICAL LINES ACROSS THESE EXTENSIONS TO REPRESENT THE TEETH STRUCTURE.

BROWS AND LASHES:

DEFINE THE BROWS USING BLACK OR DARK BROWN EYESHADOW, KEEPING THEM SUBTLE TO NOT OVERPOWER THE SKULL DESIGN. APPLY FALSE LASHES OR VOLUMIZING MASCARA TO MAKE THE EYES POP AGAINST THE HOLLOWED-OUT LOOK.

FINAL TOUCHES:

STYLE YOUR HAIR WITH VIBRANT PURPLE TONES FOR A BOLD CONTRAST TO THE MAKEUP. FINISH THE LOOK WITH A GOTHIC CHOKER AND SKELETON-INSPIRED COSTUME TO COMPLETE THE SPOOKY, YET STYLISH AESTHETIC. USE SETTING SPRAY TO KEEP THE MAKEUP IN PLACE FOR THE ENTIRE EVENT.

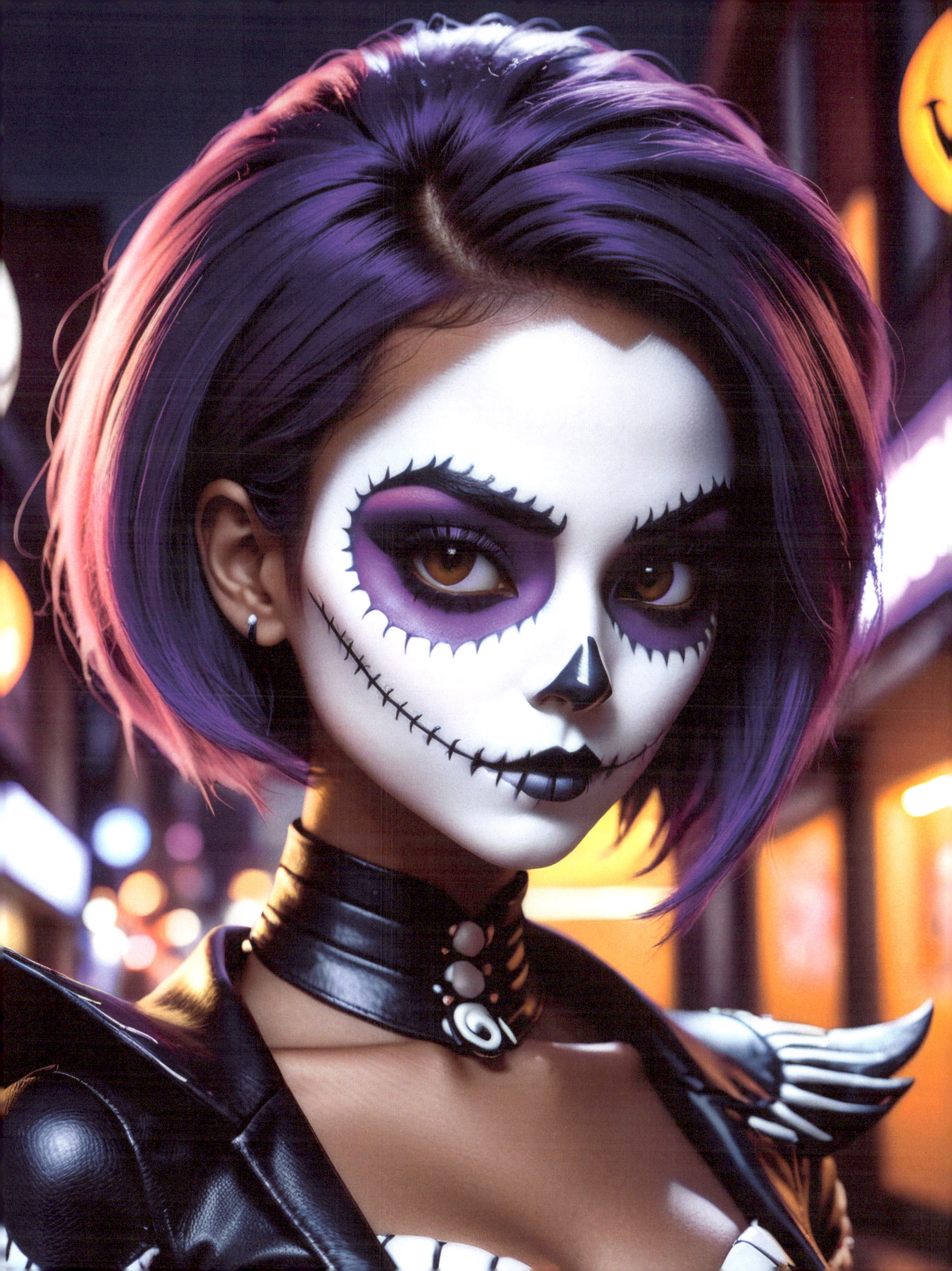

FROSTBORN DRAGON WARRIOR COSPLAY MAKEUP

STEP-BY-STEP INSTRUCTIONS:

SKIN PREPARATION:

START BY CLEANSING AND MOISTURIZING YOUR FACE. APPLY A PRIMER TO CREATE A SMOOTH BASE, FOLLOWED BY A LIGHT TO MEDIUM-COVERAGE FOUNDATION, FOCUSING ON AREAS NOT COVERED BY THE BLUE FACE PAINT.

BLUE BASE PAINT:

USE A LIGHT BLUE FACE PAINT TO COVER THE FOREHEAD, CHEEKS, AND CHIN, BLENDING SEAMLESSLY INTO YOUR NATURAL SKIN TONE. MAKE SURE THE COLOR EXTENDS AROUND THE TEMPLES AND UNDER THE CHIN FOR A FROST-LIKE EFFECT.

WHITE FROST DETAILING:

USING WHITE FACE PAINT AND A FINE BRUSH, DRAW INTRICATE, FROSTY DESIGNS AROUND THE FOREHEAD AND CHEEKS. CREATE SYMMETRICAL, ICE-LIKE PATTERNS THAT RESEMBLE FROST CRYSTALS OR SNOWFLAKES, ADDING SMALL DOTS FOR EXTRA DETAILING.

EYESHADOW AND EYELINER:

APPLY A DEEP PURPLE OR INDIGO EYESHADOW ON THE EYELIDS, BLENDING OUTWARD TO CREATE A SMOKEY, WINTERY LOOK. LINE YOUR EYES WITH BLACK EYELINER, ADDING A SLIGHT WING FOR A BOLD, ICY GAZE. USE VOLUMIZING MASCARA OR FALSE LASHES TO MAKE YOUR EYES STAND OUT.

LIPS:

APPLY A SOFT BLUE LIPSTICK TO COMPLEMENT THE FROSTY LOOK. USE A TOUCH OF WHITE LIP PAINT IN THE CENTER OF THE LIPS TO CREATE A COOL, OMBRé EFFECT, GIVING THE LIPS A FROSTED APPEARANCE.

FINAL TOUCHES:

STYLE YOUR HAIR IN SLEEK BRAIDS OR ADD EXTENSIONS TO MIMIC THE LONG, WARRIOR-LIKE STYLE. FINISH THE LOOK WITH HORNED ACCESSORIES AND SILVER ARMOR FOR A FIERCE, DRAGON-INSPIRED WARRIOR AESTHETIC. SET THE MAKEUP WITH A SETTING SPRAY TO ENSURE LONG-LASTING WEAR IN ALL CONDITIONS.

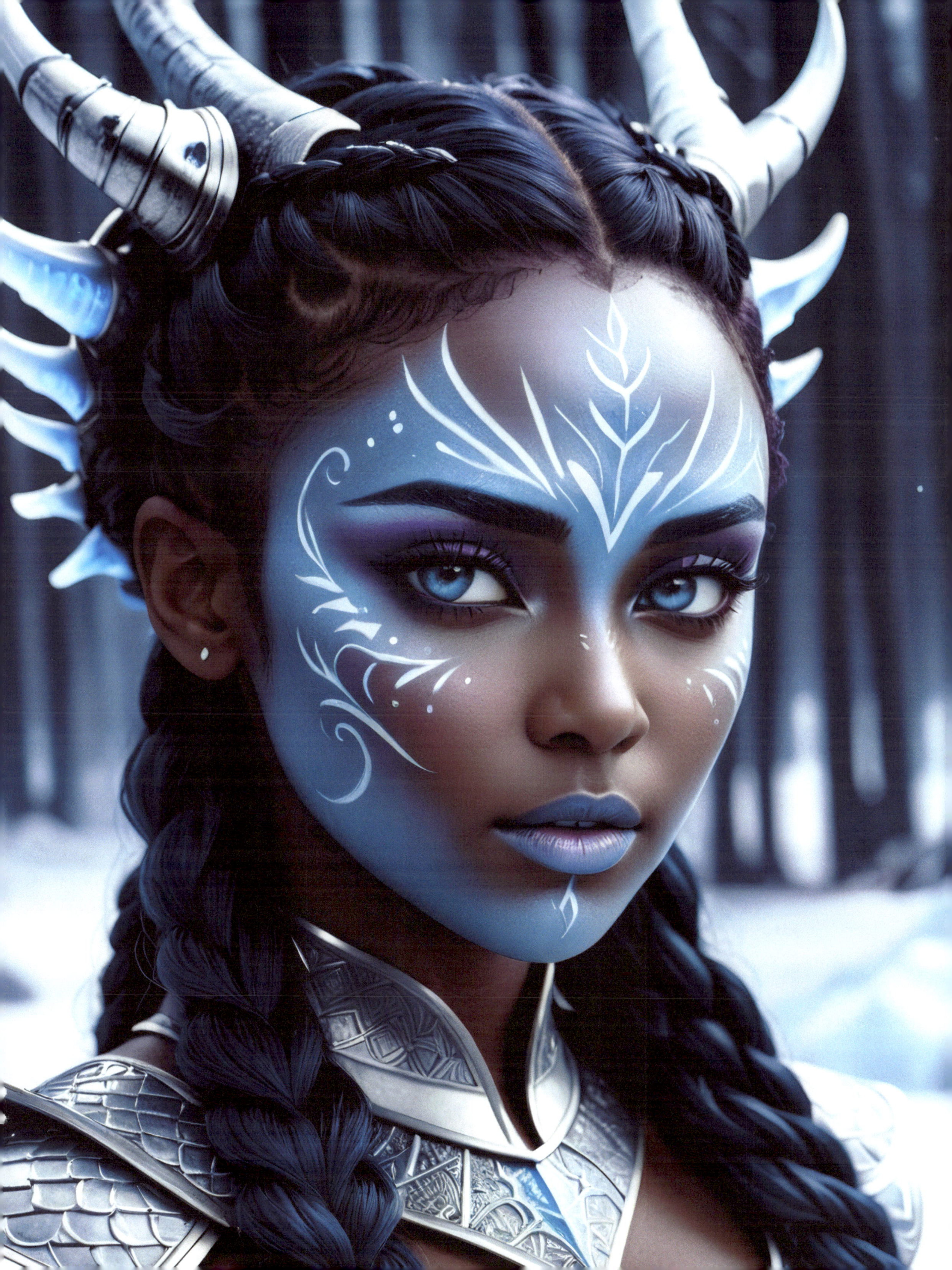

GALACTIC WARRIOR COSPLAY MAKEUP

STEP-BY-STEP INSTRUCTIONS:

SKIN PREPARATION:

CLEANSE AND MOISTURIZE YOUR FACE FOR A SMOOTH CANVAS. APPLY A PRIMER TO PROLONG THE MAKEUP'S WEAR, FOLLOWED BY A LIGHT FOUNDATION TO EVEN OUT YOUR SKIN TONE WHILE FOCUSING ON AREAS NOT COVERED BY THE FACE PAINT.

RED AND WHITE TRIBAL FACE PAINT:

USING WHITE FACE PAINT, CREATE BOLD SYMMETRICAL PATTERNS ALONG THE CHEEKS, FOREHEAD, AND NOSE. ADD RED ACCENTS OVER THE WHITE TO FORM DYNAMIC SHAPES THAT MIRROR WARRIOR MARKINGS. USE A FINE BRUSH FOR PRECISE LINES AND GEOMETRIC DETAILING.

EYESHADOW AND EYELINER:

APPLY A BRIGHT RED EYESHADOW ON THE LIDS, BLENDING OUTWARDS FOR A FIERCE LOOK. LINE YOUR UPPER AND LOWER LASH LINES WITH BLACK EYELINER, CREATING A SHARP WING FOR A BOLD, INTENSE GAZE. APPLY FALSE LASHES OR VOLUMIZING MASCARA TO ENHANCE THE EYES.

BROWS AND LASHES:

DEFINE THE BROWS USING A BROW PENCIL, SHAPING THEM NATURALLY TO BALANCE THE BOLD FACE PAINT. FOR EXTRA INTENSITY, APPLY SEVERAL COATS OF MASCARA OR FALSE LASHES TO GIVE THE EYES A MORE DRAMATIC EFFECT.

LIPS:

OPT FOR A BRIGHT RED MATTE LIPSTICK TO COMPLEMENT THE RED ACCENTS IN THE FACE PAINT, ENSURING CLEAN, SHARP LINES WITH A MATCHING LIP LINER FOR DEFINITION.

FINAL TOUCHES:

STYLE YOUR HAIR WITH INTRICATE BRAIDED DESIGNS, ADDING RED ACCENTS OR EXTENSIONS TO MATCH THE WARRIOR THEME. COMPLETE THE LOOK WITH ARMOR-INSPIRED ACCESSORIES AND SHOULDER PIECES. SET THE MAKEUP WITH A SETTING SPRAY FOR DURABILITY THROUGHOUT YOUR EVENT OR COSPLAY GATHERING.

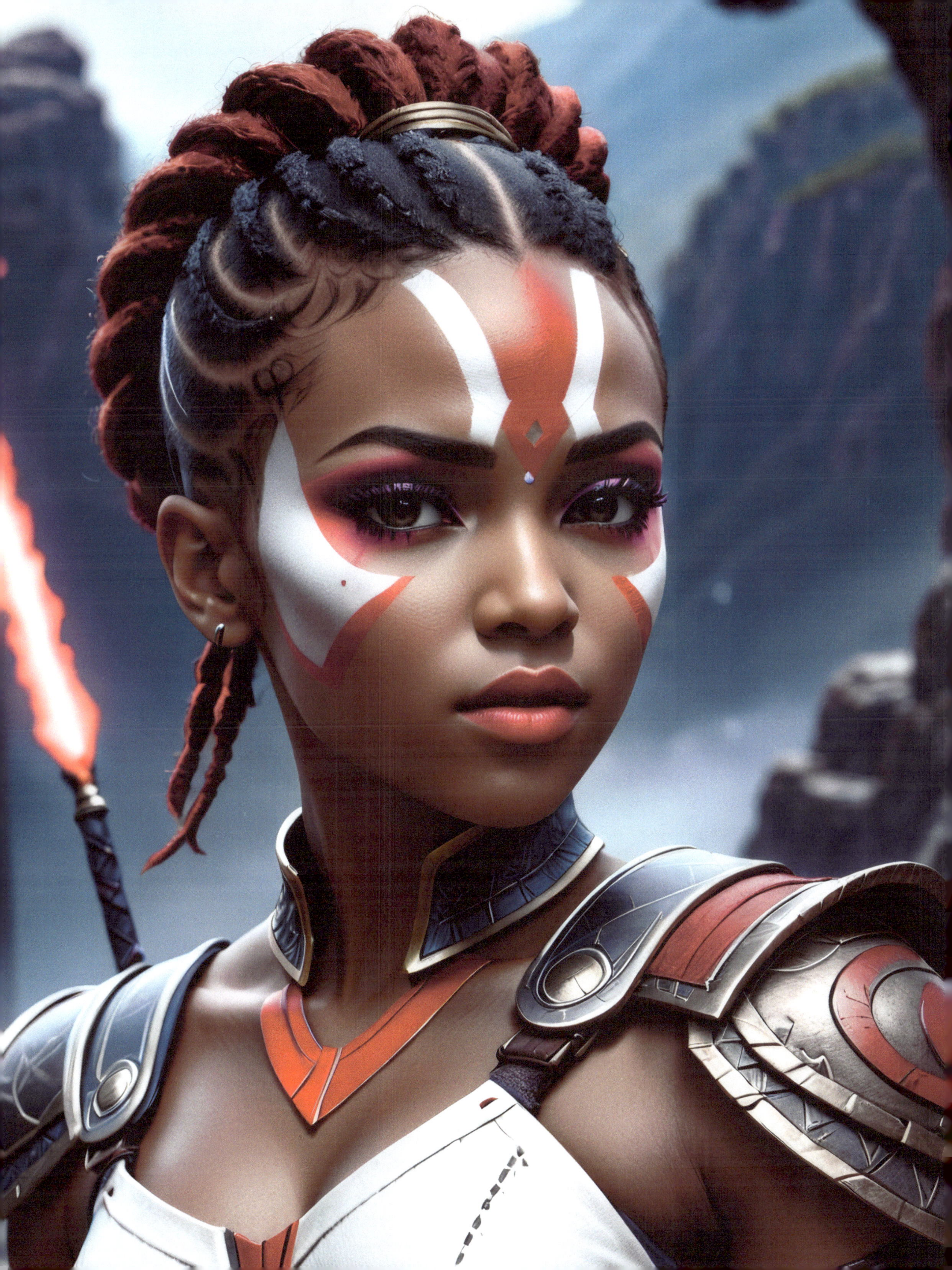

MONOCHROME PHANTOM COSPLAY MAKEUP

STEP-BY-STEP INSTRUCTIONS:

SKIN PREPARATION:

BEGIN BY CLEANSING AND MOISTURIZING YOUR FACE. APPLY A PRIMER TO ENSURE SMOOTH MAKEUP APPLICATION. USE A LIGHT FOUNDATION ON THE AREAS NOT COVERED BY FACE PAINT TO EVEN OUT THE SKIN TONE.

WHITE BASE PAINT:

COVER THE ENTIRE FACE WITH A WHITE FACE PAINT USING A MAKEUP SPONGE OR BRUSH. FOCUS ON ACHIEVING A SMOOTH AND EVEN FINISH, BLENDING INTO THE HAIRLINE AND JAWLINE FOR A FLAWLESS BASE.

BLACK EYE AND FACE DETAILS:

USING BLACK FACE PAINT, CREATE A DRAMATIC MASK-LIKE DESIGN AROUND THE EYES, COVERING THE EYELIDS AND EXTENDING OUTWARD. ADD A LARGE, ABSTRACT SHAPE ON ONE SIDE OF THE FACE FOR AN ASYMMETRICAL, ARTISTIC EFFECT.

EYESHADOW AND EYELINER:

APPLY BLACK EYESHADOW TO INTENSIFY THE AREAS AROUND THE EYES, BLENDING FOR A SMOKY, DEEP LOOK. LINE THE UPPER AND LOWER LASH LINES WITH BLACK EYELINER FOR SHARP DEFINITION, AND ADD MASCARA FOR EXTRA EMPHASIS ON THE LASHES.

LIPS:

USE A DEEP, RICH RED OR BLACK LIPSTICK TO CREATE A BOLD CONTRAST WITH THE WHITE BASE. OUTLINE THE LIPS WITH A MATCHING LIP LINER FOR PRECISE, CLEAN EDGES, ENSURING THE LIPS POP AGAINST THE MONOCHROMATIC MAKEUP.

FINAL TOUCHES:

STYLE YOUR HAIR WITH SOFT, FLOWING WAVES OR WEAR A WHITE WIG TO MATCH THE DRAMATIC MONOCHROME LOOK. ADD A BLACK LEATHER CHOKER FOR A GOTHIC TOUCH, AND SET THE ENTIRE MAKEUP WITH A SETTING SPRAY TO ENSURE LONG-LASTING WEAR

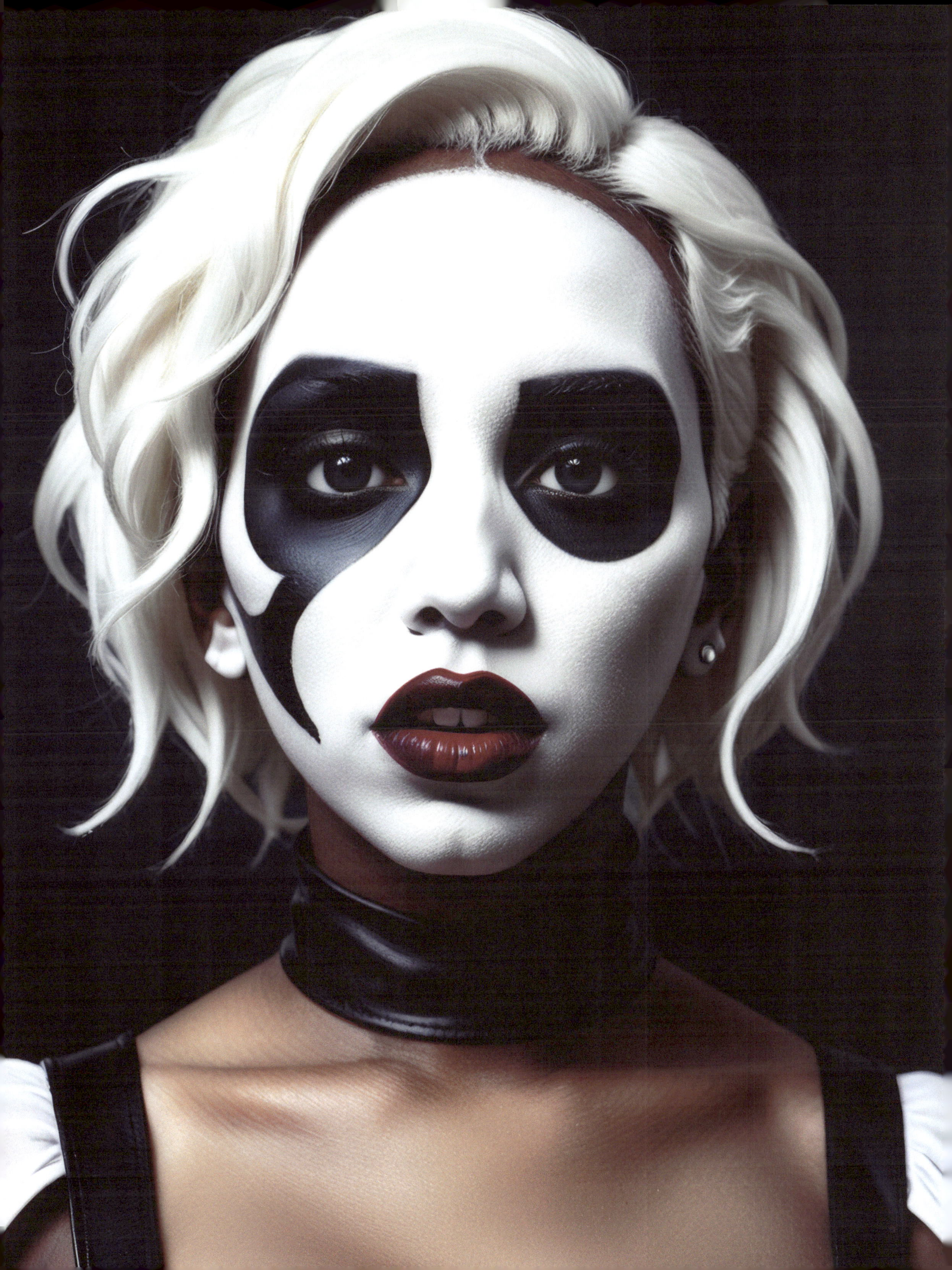

TRIBAL HUNTRESS COSPLAY MAKEUP

SSTEP-BY-STEP INSTRUCTIONS:

SKIN PREPARATION:

START BY CLEANSING AND MOISTURIZING YOUR FACE. APPLY A PRIMER TO ENSURE LONG-LASTING WEAR. FOLLOW WITH A LIGHT FOUNDATION, FOCUSING ON EVENING OUT YOUR SKIN TONE WHILE LEAVING SPACE FOR THE FACE PAINT.

WHITE TRIBAL MARKINGS:

USE WHITE FACE PAINT TO CREATE INTRICATE TRIBAL PATTERNS ACROSS THE FOREHEAD, CHEEKS, AND UNDER THE EYES. FOCUS ON SYMMETRY AND SHARP LINES, FORMING GEOMETRIC SHAPES AND DOTS TO MIMIC TRADITIONAL TRIBAL SYMBOLS.

DARK EYESHADOW AND CONTOUR:

APPLY A DEEP PURPLE OR BLACK EYESHADOW AROUND THE EYES, EXTENDING IT OUTWARD FOR A SMOKY EFFECT. BLEND CAREFULLY TO CONTRAST AGAINST THE WHITE MARKINGS, CREATING A DRAMATIC EYE LOOK. LIGHTLY CONTOUR THE CHEEKS WITH BRONZER TO DEFINE THE FACE.

EYEBROWS AND EYELINER:

SHAPE AND FILL IN YOUR BROWS WITH A DARK BROW PENCIL, KEEPING THEM NATURAL YET DEFINED. USE BLACK EYELINER TO ACCENTUATE THE LASH LINE AND ADD A SUBTLE WING FOR EXTRA INTENSITY. FOLLOW UP WITH VOLUMIZING MASCARA OR FALSE LASHES FOR BOLD, CAPTIVATING EYES.

LIPS:

KEEP THE LIPS NEUTRAL WITH A SOFT PINK OR NUDE LIPSTICK TO BALANCE THE BOLD EYE AND FACE PAINT. FOR A FULLER LOOK, USE A MATCHING LIP LINER TO DEFINE THE EDGES.

FINAL TOUCHES:

STYLE YOUR HAIR WITH BRAIDS OR ADD GREEN AND BLUE HAIR EXTENSIONS TO ENHANCE THE HUNTRESS THEME. FINISH THE LOOK WITH METALLIC ACCESSORIES SUCH AS A CHOKER OR PENDANT THAT MATCH THE TRIBAL AESTHETIC. SET THE MAKEUP WITH A SETTING SPRAY TO KEEP EVERYTHING INTACT THROUGHOUT YOUR EVENT.

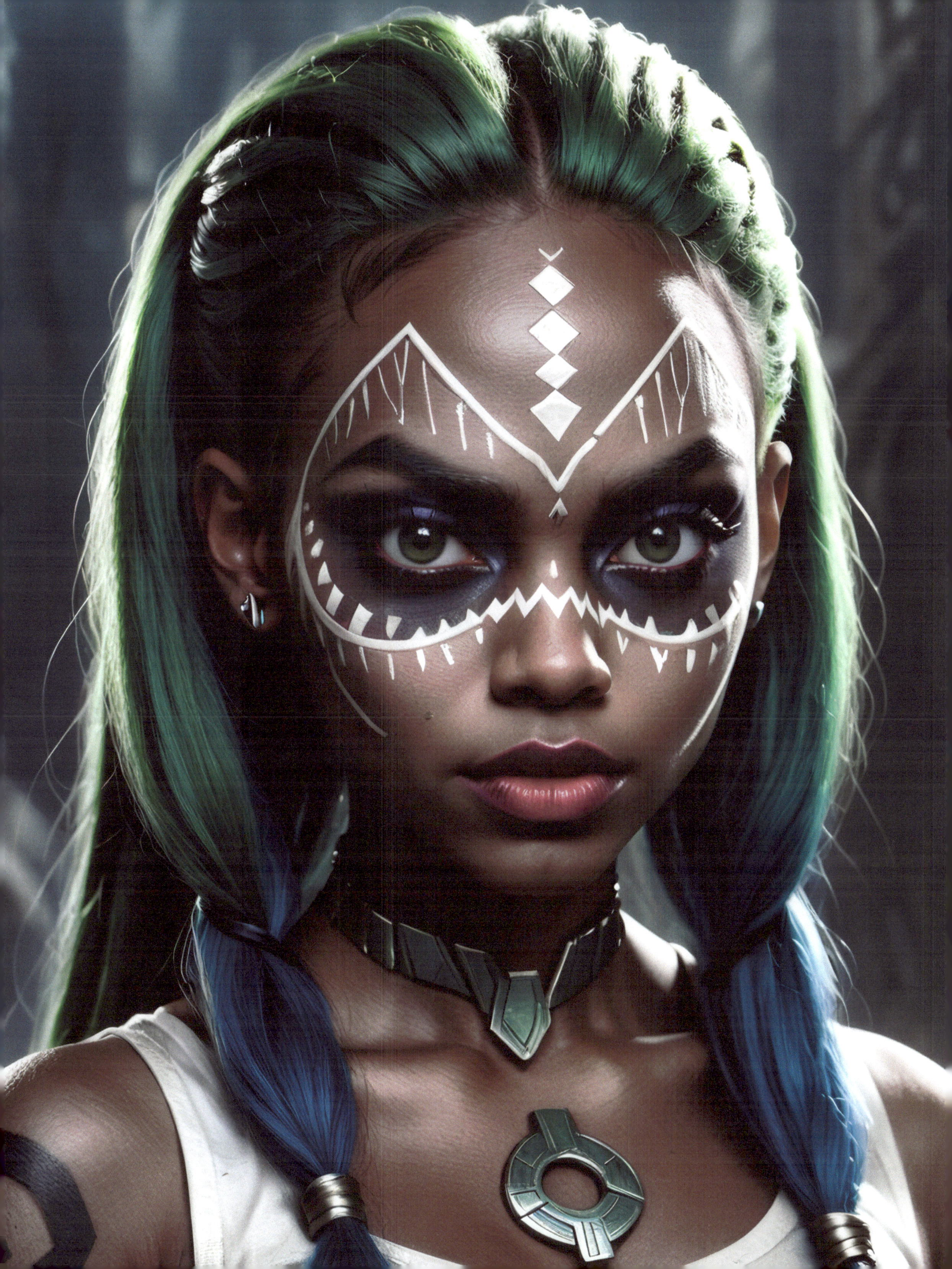

FUTURISTIC MASKED COSPLAY MAKEUP

STEP-BY-STEP INSTRUCTIONS:

SKIN PREPARATION:

START BY CLEANSING AND MOISTURIZING YOUR FACE TO CREATE A SMOOTH CANVAS. APPLY A PRIMER TO ENSURE LONGEVITY AND FOLLOW WITH A FOUNDATION THAT MATCHES YOUR SKIN TONE, FOCUSING ON THE UPPER PART OF YOUR FACE NOT COVERED BY THE WHITE MASK.

WHITE MASK BASE:

USE WHITE FACE PAINT TO CREATE A SLEEK MASK-LIKE SHAPE THAT COVERS THE LOWER HALF OF YOUR FACE, FROM THE NOSE DOWN TO THE CHIN. USE A MAKEUP SPONGE OR BRUSH TO ACHIEVE AN EVEN, SEAMLESS APPLICATION. BLEND THE EDGES CAREFULLY FOR A CLEAN FINISH.

EYESHADOW AND EYELINER:

APPLY BOLD PURPLE EYESHADOW, BLENDING IT ACROSS THE LIDS AND SLIGHTLY OUTWARD FOR A DRAMATIC LOOK. USE A BLACK EYELINER TO CREATE A SHARP LINE ALONG THE UPPER LASH LINE, EXTENDING INTO A WING. FINISH WITH FALSE LASHES OR SEVERAL COATS OF VOLUMIZING MASCARA TO MAKE THE EYES STAND OUT.

BROWS AND LASHES:

SHAPE AND FILL IN YOUR BROWS USING A DARK BROW PENCIL TO CREATE A DEFINED LOOK THAT BALANCES THE BOLD EYE MAKEUP. APPLY MASCARA TO THE LOWER LASHES FOR A POLISHED FINISH.

LIPS:

PAINT THE LIPS WITH THE SAME WHITE FACE PAINT USED FOR THE MASK, ENSURING CLEAN AND SHARP EDGES FOR A FUTURISTIC, MINIMALIST VIBE. ALTERNATIVELY, YOU CAN USE A PALE, MATTE LIP COLOR TO BLEND WITH THE MASK SEAMLESSLY.

FINAL TOUCHES:

STYLE YOUR HAIR WITH SOFT WAVES OR WEAR A WIG WITH PURPLE HIGHLIGHTS FOR A VIBRANT, CONTRASTING EFFECT. ADD A WHITE HAT OR ACCESSORIES TO ENHANCE THE FUTURISTIC, SLEEK LOOK. SET THE MAKEUP WITH SETTING SPRAY TO ENSURE IT LASTS THROUGHOUT THE EVENT OR COSPLAY.

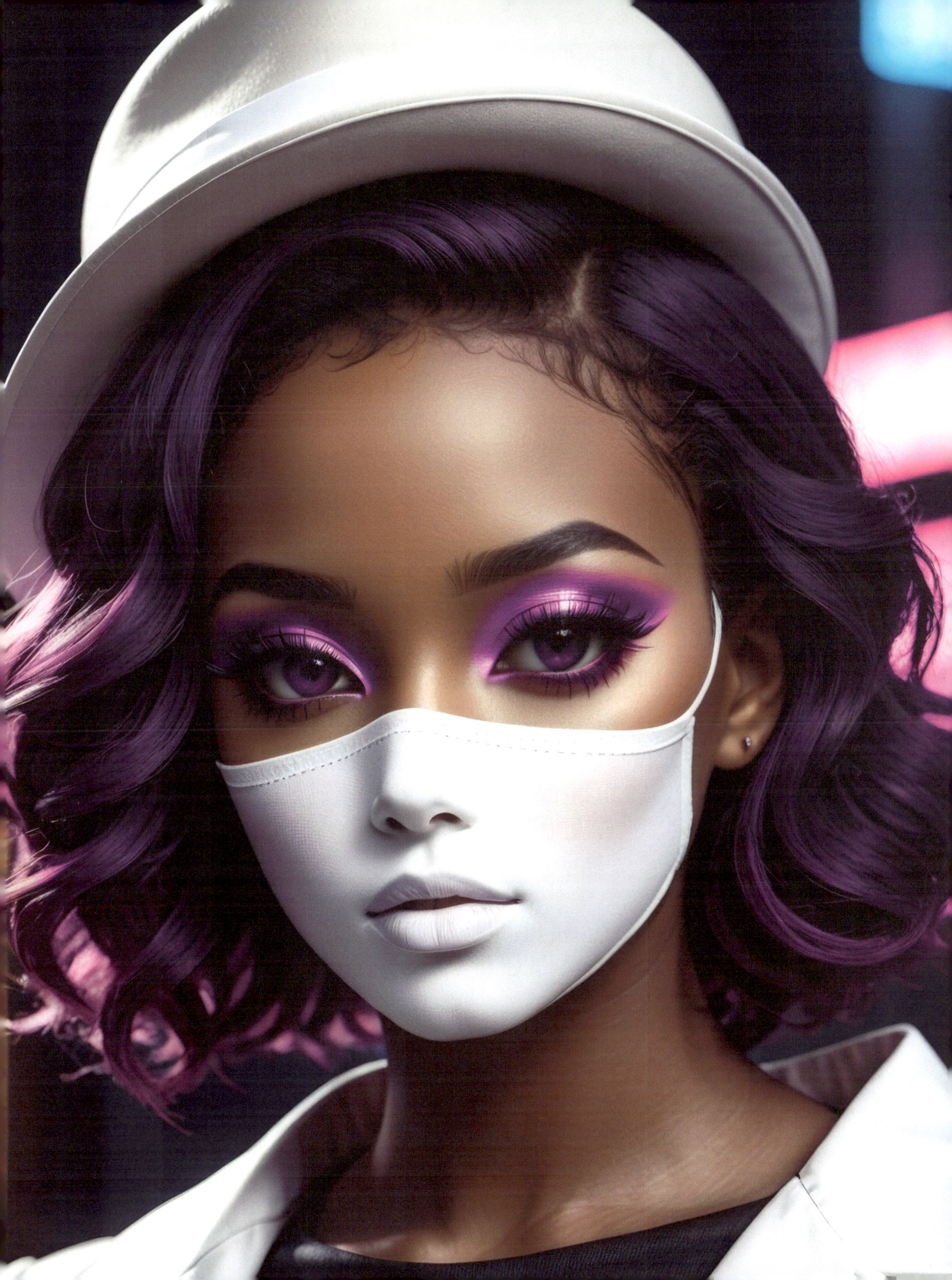

BLOODSTAINED MASK COSPLAY MAKEUP

STEP-BY-STEP INSTRUCTIONS:

SKIN PREPARATION:

BEGIN BY CLEANSING AND MOISTURIZING YOUR SKIN. APPLY A PRIMER FOR SMOOTH APPLICATION, FOLLOWED BY FOUNDATION ON AREAS NOT COVERED BY THE FACE PAINT. ENSURE AN EVEN, FLAWLESS BASE.

WHITE MASK BASE:

COVER YOUR FACE WITH WHITE FACE PAINT, FOCUSING ON CREATING SHARP, DEFINED EDGES ALONG THE FOREHEAD, CHEEKS, AND CHIN TO MIMIC A MASK-LIKE EFFECT. USE A MAKEUP SPONGE OR BRUSH FOR A SEAMLESS FINISH.

BLOOD EFFECTS:

APPLY DEEP RED FACE PAINT OR SPECIAL EFFECTS MAKEUP TO CREATE BLOOD-LIKE STREAKS. FOCUS ON ADDING DRAMATIC BLOOD DRIPS ALONG THE FOREHEAD AND UNDER THE EYES, SIMULATING A MASK THAT IS CRACKING OR BLEEDING. FOR EXTRA REALISM, ADD SOME SHINE TO THE "BLOOD" USING GLOSS OR A GEL-BASED PRODUCT.

EYESHADOW AND LINER:

APPLY DARK, SMOKY EYESHADOW AROUND THE EYES, BLENDING IT OUTWARD TO CREATE A HOLLOWED EFFECT. USE BLACK EYELINER TO DEFINE THE UPPER AND LOWER LASH LINES, AND APPLY FALSE LASHES OR VOLUMIZING MASCARA TO INTENSIFY THE EYES.

LIPS:

USE A DEEP RED LIPSTICK TO MATCH THE BLOOD ACCENTS, KEEPING THE LIP SHAPE SHARP AND WELL-DEFINED. YOU CAN ADD A TOUCH OF GLOSS TO ENHANCE THE BOLD LOOK.

FINAL TOUCHES:

STYLE YOUR HAIR WITH LOOSE, CONTROLLED WAVES TO FRAME THE FACE AND MAINTAIN THE FOCUS ON THE MASK DESIGN. FINISH WITH A SETTING SPRAY TO ENSURE THE MAKEUP STAYS INTACT THROUGHOUT THE EVENT OR COSPLAY PERFORMANCE.

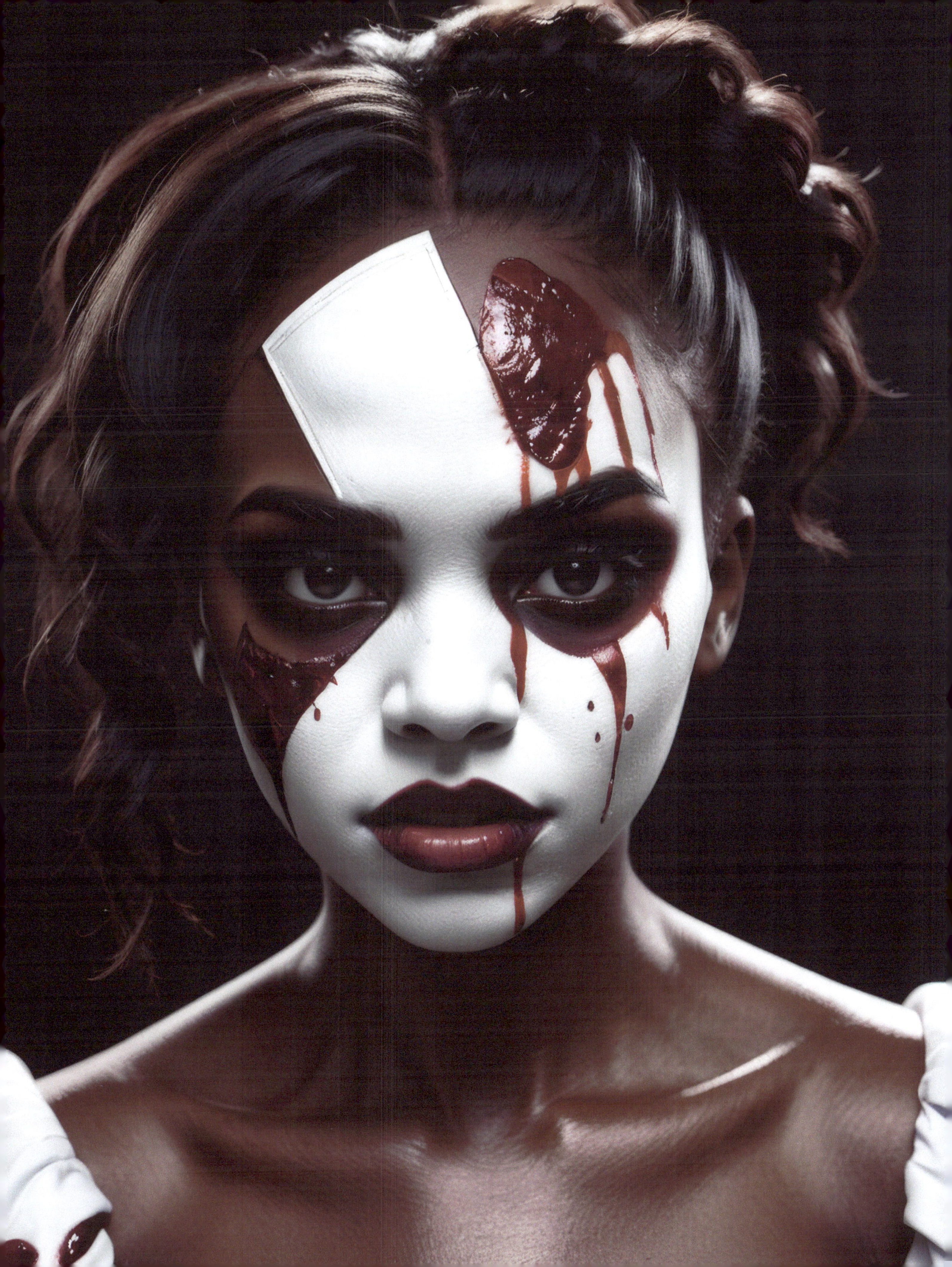

FUTURISTIC ORANGE CYBORG COSPLAY MAKEUP

STEP-BY-STEP INSTRUCTIONS:

SKIN PREPARATION:

START BY CLEANSING AND MOISTURIZING YOUR SKIN. APPLY A PRIMER TO CREATE A SMOOTH BASE, FOLLOWED BY A LIGHT FOUNDATION TO EVEN OUT YOUR SKIN TONE, FOCUSING ON AREAS NOT COVERED BY THE FACE PAINT.

WHITE AND ORANGE FACE PAINT:

USE WHITE FACE PAINT TO COVER MOST OF THE FACE, LEAVING SPACE FOR THE ORANGE DETAILING AROUND THE EYES AND MOUTH. APPLY THE ORANGE PAINT IN A FUTURISTIC MASK-LIKE SHAPE AROUND THE EYES AND MOUTH, BLENDING SMOOTHLY WITH THE WHITE BASE. USE A FINE BRUSH FOR CLEAN, DEFINED EDGES.

EYESHADOW AND EYELINER:

APPLY ORANGE EYESHADOW ON THE LIDS, BLENDING IT UPWARDS TOWARD THE BROW BONE FOR A COHESIVE LOOK WITH THE FACE PAINT. USE BLACK EYELINER TO DEFINE THE UPPER LASH LINE, KEEPING THE LINER THIN TO MAINTAIN THE FUTURISTIC AESTHETIC. FINISH WITH MASCARA TO ADD VOLUME TO THE LASHES.

EYEBROWS AND LIPS:

SHAPE AND FILL IN YOUR EYEBROWS WITH A DARK BROW PENCIL FOR A BOLD AND DEFINED LOOK. USE AN ORANGE LIPSTICK TO MATCH THE FACE PAINT, MAKING SURE THE LIPS ARE PRECISELY LINED FOR A CLEAN, ROBOTIC APPEARANCE.

FRECKLES AND DETAIL WORK:

ADD SMALL BLACK DOTS OR FRECKLES AROUND THE CHEEKS AND NOSE TO MIMIC FUTURISTIC DETAILING, USING A FINE BRUSH OR BLACK EYELINER. THESE ADD SUBTLE TEXTURE AND DEPTH TO THE OVERALL LOOK.

FINAL TOUCHES:

STYLE YOUR HAIR WITH A STRAIGHT ORANGE WIG OR ADD ORANGE EXTENSIONS TO MATCH THE THEME. COMPLETE THE LOOK WITH A SLEEK, METALLIC OUTFIT AND ACCESSORIES LIKE A CHOKER TO ENHANCE THE CYBERNETIC, FUTURISTIC VIBE. USE A SETTING SPRAY TO ENSURE THE MAKEUP LASTS THROUGHOUT YOUR EVENT OR PHOTOSHOOT.

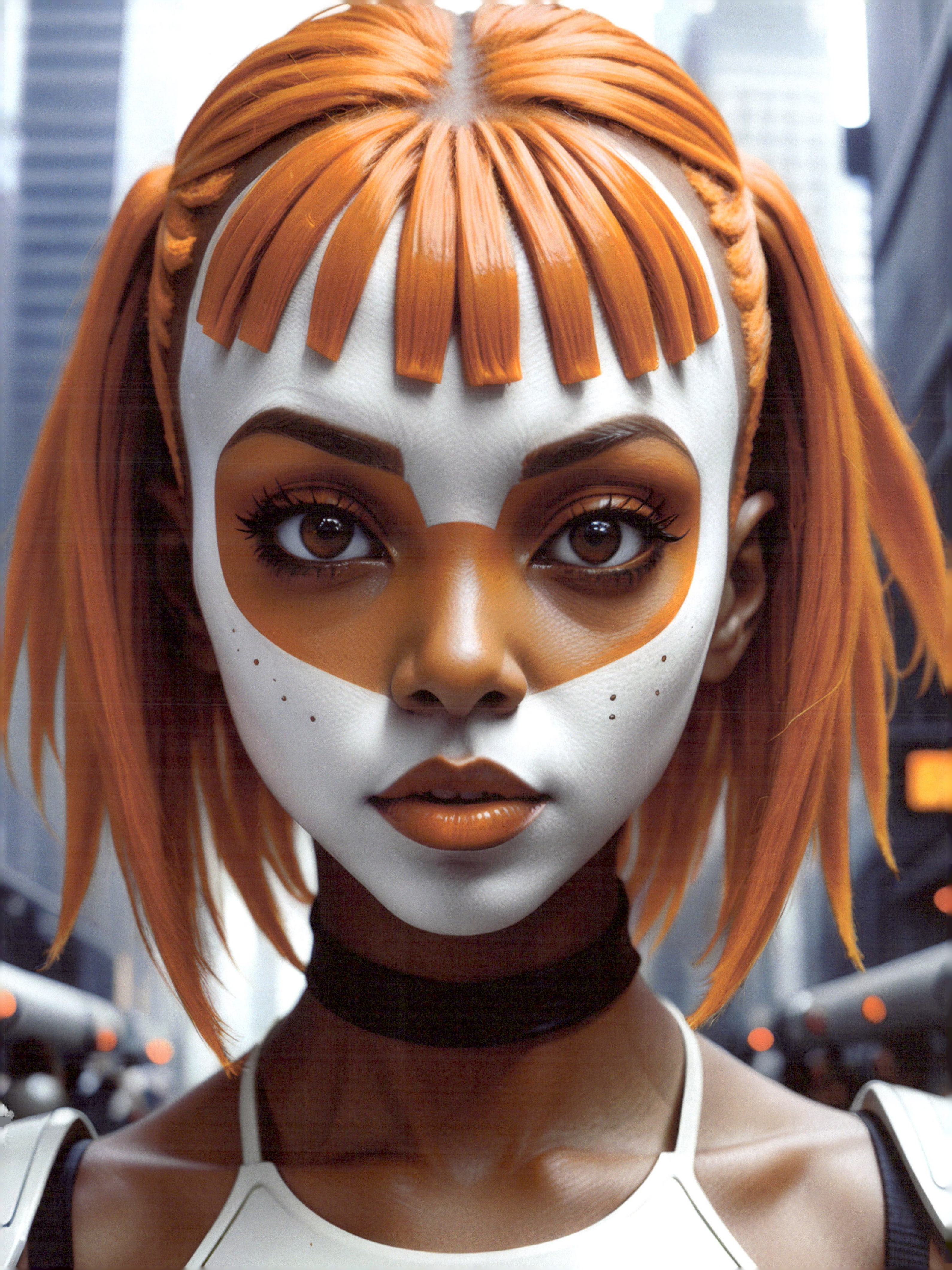

CIRCUS CLOWN COSPLAY MAKEUP

STEP-BY-STEP INSTRUCTIONS:

SKIN PREPARATION:

START BY CLEANSING AND MOISTURIZING YOUR SKIN. APPLY A PRIMER FOR SMOOTH APPLICATION AND LONG-LASTING MAKEUP. USE A FOUNDATION ON AREAS NOT COVERED BY FACE PAINT TO CREATE AN EVEN SKIN TONE.

WHITE FACE PAINT BASE:

COVER THE ENTIRE FACE WITH WHITE FACE PAINT, USING A MAKEUP SPONGE OR BRUSH FOR A SMOOTH, EVEN FINISH. ENSURE THE EDGES ARE WELL BLENDED AROUND THE HAIRLINE AND JAWLINE.

CLOWN MARKINGS:

USING RED FACE PAINT, DRAW A CIRCLE ON THE NOSE AND TWO SMALLER CIRCLES ON THE FOREHEAD AND CHEEKS. FOR THE EYES, USE PURPLE EYESHADOW AROUND THE LIDS AND ADD BLUE TEAR-SHAPED LINES EXTENDING DOWNWARDS FROM THE LOWER LASH LINE. ADD A CURVED RED LINE EXTENDING FROM THE CORNERS OF THE MOUTH FOR A CLASSIC CLOWN SMILE.

EYESHADOW AND LINER:

APPLY BOLD PURPLE EYESHADOW ON THE LIDS, BLENDING IT UPWARDS TOWARD THE BROW BONE. USE BLACK EYELINER TO DEFINE THE EYES, CREATING SHARP, WINGED LINES. ADD FALSE LASHES OR SEVERAL COATS OF VOLUMIZING MASCARA FOR A DRAMATIC EYE LOOK.

LIPS:

OUTLINE AND FILL IN THE LIPS WITH RED LIPSTICK TO MATCH THE CLOWN THEME. ENSURE CLEAN AND SHARP EDGES TO CONTRAST AGAINST THE WHITE FACE PAINT, ADDING TO THE STRIKING CLOWNISH APPEARANCE.

FINAL TOUCHES:

STYLE YOUR HAIR WITH VOLUMINOUS PIGTAILS OR ADD COLORFUL EXTENSIONS, LIKE PURPLE DREADLOCKS, FOR A PLAYFUL, CIRCUS-INSPIRED LOOK. COMPLETE THE OUTFIT WITH A CLASSIC CLOWN COSTUME, INCLUDING A RUFFLED COLLAR AND BRIGHT ACCESSORIES. SET THE MAKEUP WITH A SETTING SPRAY TO ENSURE IT STAYS IN PLACE THROUGHOUT THE EVENT OR PERFORMANCE.

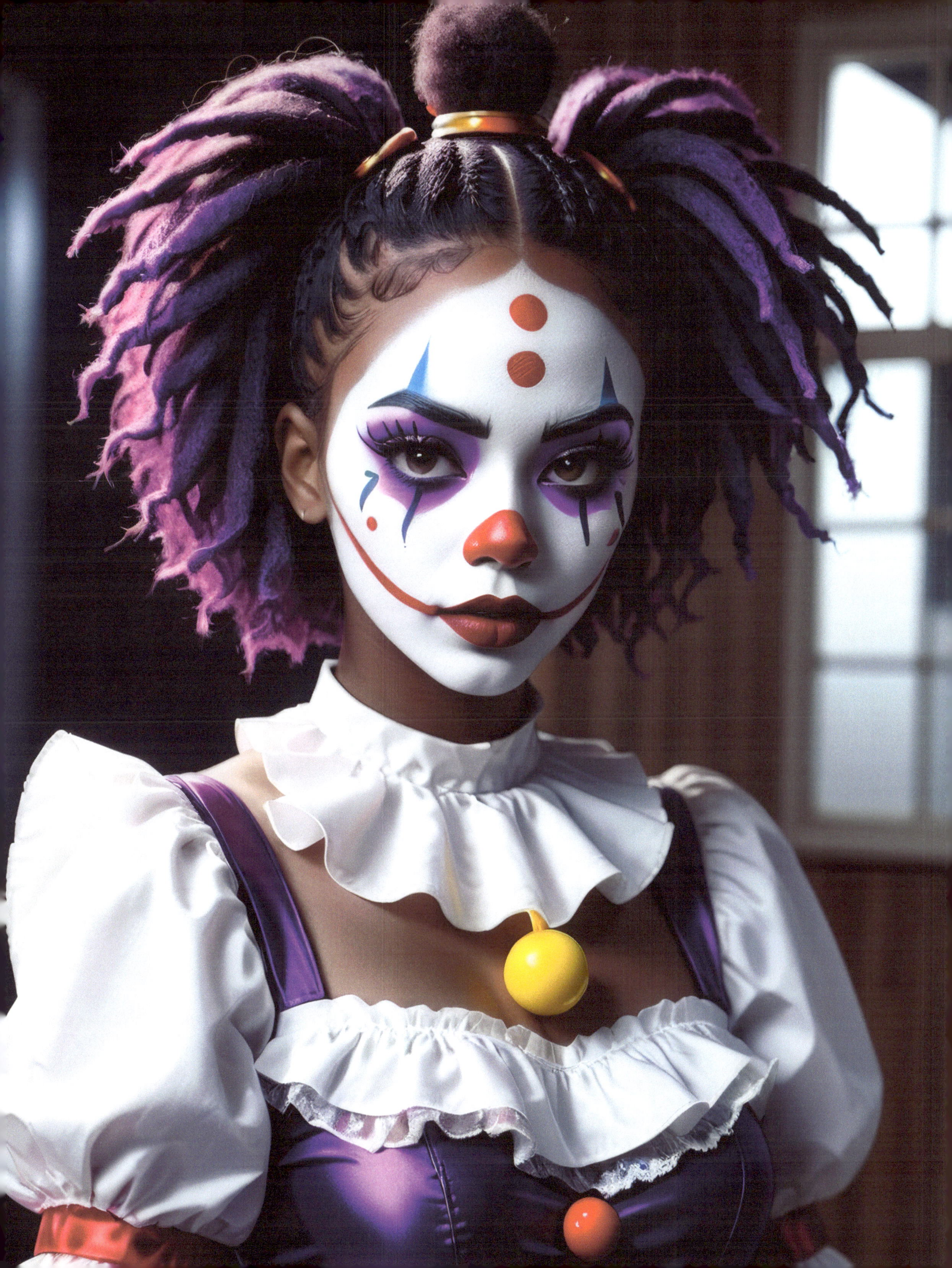

HAUNTED DOLL COSPLAY MAKEUP

STEP-BY-STEP INSTRUCTIONS:

SKIN PREPARATION:

START BY CLEANSING AND MOISTURIZING YOUR SKIN. APPLY A PRIMER FOR SMOOTH APPLICATION AND USE A LIGHT FOUNDATION WHERE NEEDED, LEAVING SPACE FOR THE WHITE FACE PAINT.

WHITE BASE PAINT:

APPLY WHITE FACE PAINT ALL OVER THE FACE, FOCUSING ON CREATING AN EVEN, MASK-LIKE FINISH. USE A MAKEUP SPONGE OR BRUSH TO ENSURE A SMOOTH APPLICATION, BLENDING AROUND THE HAIRLINE AND JAWLINE FOR A SEAMLESS LOOK.

BLOOD AND STITCH DETAILS:

USE RED FACE PAINT OR SPECIAL EFFECTS MAKEUP TO CREATE VERTICAL STITCH-LIKE MARKS ON THE FOREHEAD AND CHEEKS. ADD SMALL DROPLETS OF "BLOOD" DRIPPING FROM THE STITCHES FOR A REALISTIC, HAUNTING EFFECT. FOR ADDED TEXTURE, USE BLACK FACE PAINT TO CREATE A CROSS-HATCHED EFFECT OVER THE "WOUNDS."

DARK EYESHADOW AND LINER:

APPLY BLACK OR DEEP BURGUNDY EYESHADOW AROUND THE EYES, EXTENDING IT INTO A SMOKY, HOLLOWED EFFECT. USE BLACK EYELINER TO DEFINE THE UPPER AND LOWER LASH LINES, CREATING A SHARP, INTENSE LOOK. ADD MASCARA OR FALSE LASHES TO INTENSIFY THE EYES FURTHER.

LIPS:

USE A DEEP RED OR BURGUNDY LIPSTICK TO CREATE A HAUNTING, DOLL-LIKE APPEARANCE. FOR AN EERIE TOUCH, ADD A SMALL RED DRIP EXTENDING FROM THE LOWER LIP, MIMICKING BLOOD.

FINAL TOUCHES:

STYLE YOUR HAIR IN SOFT, LOOSE CURLS OR WAVES TO CONTRAST THE HAUNTING MAKEUP. ADD SPECIAL EFFECTS LIKE FAKE BLOOD ON THE NECK OR CHEST TO ENHANCE THE EERIE LOOK, AND FINISH WITH A SETTING SPRAY TO KEEP THE MAKEUP IN PLACE THROUGHOUT YOUR EVENT.

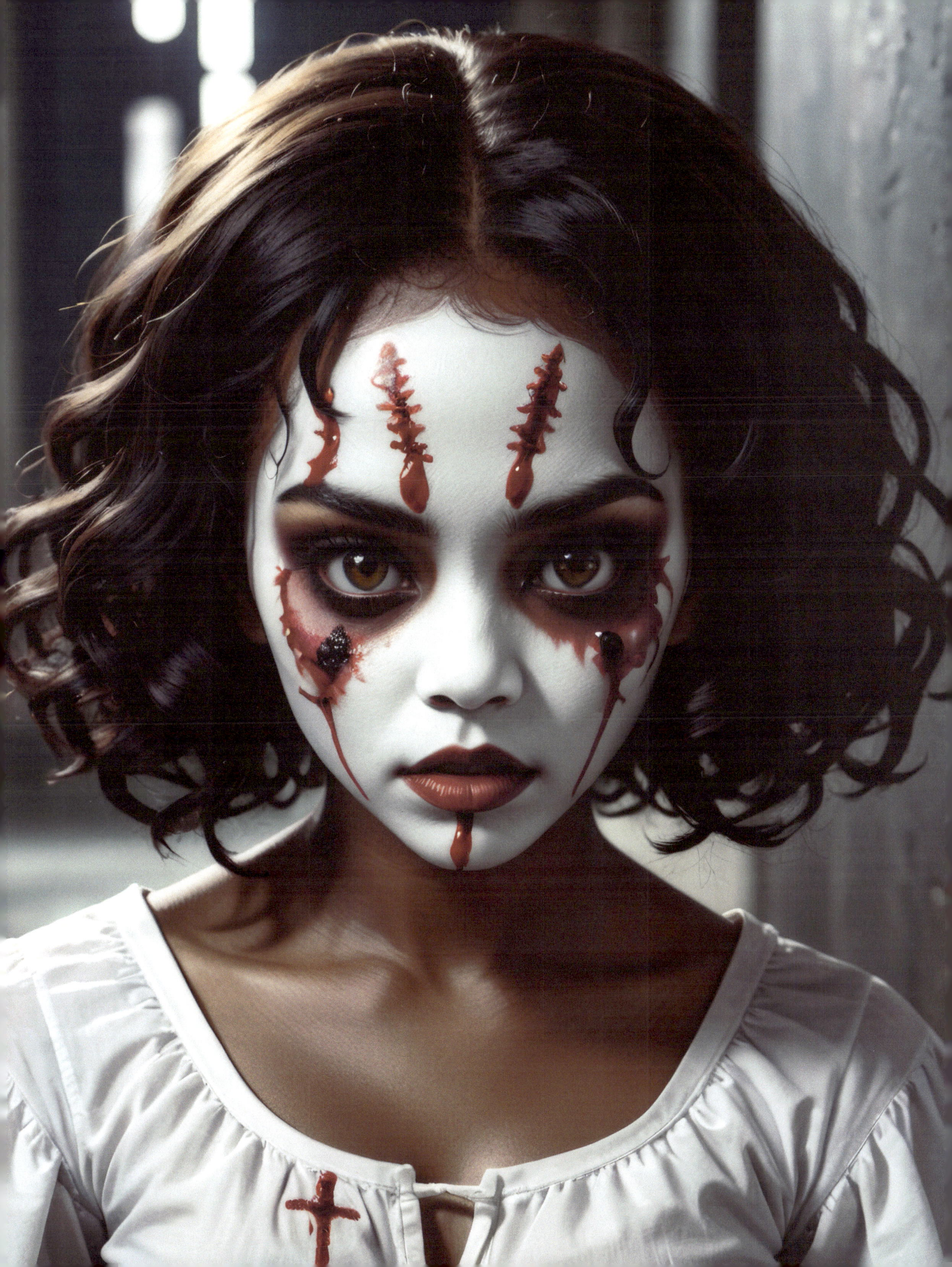

GOTHIC VAMPIRE QUEEN COSPLAY MAKEUP

STEP-BY-STEP INSTRUCTIONS:

SKIN PREPARATION:

START BY CLEANSING AND MOISTURIZING YOUR FACE TO CREATE A SMOOTH CANVAS. APPLY A PRIMER TO ENSURE LONG-LASTING MAKEUP. USE A LIGHT FOUNDATION TO COVER AREAS THAT WON'T BE PAINTED WHITE.

WHITE BASE PAINT:

COVER THE ENTIRE FACE WITH A SMOOTH LAYER OF WHITE FACE PAINT, LEAVING THE FOREHEAD AND UPPER CHEEKS FOR DETAILED BLACK SHADING. ENSURE THAT THE EDGES ARE SHARP AND CLEAN, ESPECIALLY AROUND THE HAIRLINE AND NECK.

EYESHADOW AND SMOKEY EYES:

APPLY DEEP BLACK AND BURGUNDY EYESHADOW AROUND THE EYES TO CREATE A DRAMATIC SMOKEY EYE EFFECT. BLEND THE EYESHADOW INTO THE LOWER LASH LINE TO ADD DEPTH AND INTENSITY. USE BLACK EYELINER TO CREATE THIN, SHARP LINES EXTENDING FROM THE LOWER LASH LINE, MIMICKING CRACKS OR TEARS.

BLOOD RED ACCENTS:

USING RED FACE PAINT, CREATE SMALL CROSS-LIKE DETAILS ON THE FOREHEAD AND AROUND THE EYES. THE RED ACCENTS ADD AN OMINOUS, VAMPIRIC FEEL TO THE MAKEUP AND ENHANCE THE DARK, GOTHIC LOOK.

LIPS:

APPLY DEEP, MATTE RED LIPSTICK TO ACHIEVE A VAMPIRIC ALLURE. FOR ADDED PRECISION, USE A LIP LINER TO OUTLINE THE LIPS FIRST, ENSURING SHARP, DEFINED EDGES THAT COMPLEMENT THE DARK, GOTHIC THEME.

FINAL TOUCHES:

STYLE YOUR HAIR IN ELEGANT WAVES OR CURLS, OR OPT FOR A SLEEK, PINNED-BACK LOOK TO COMPLEMENT THE REGAL, VAMPIRE AESTHETIC. COMPLETE THE LOOK WITH A BLACK, GOTHIC CHOKER OR NECKLACE, AND FINISH WITH SETTING SPRAY TO LOCK THE MAKEUP IN PLACE FOR A LONG-LASTING, DRAMATIC EFFECT.

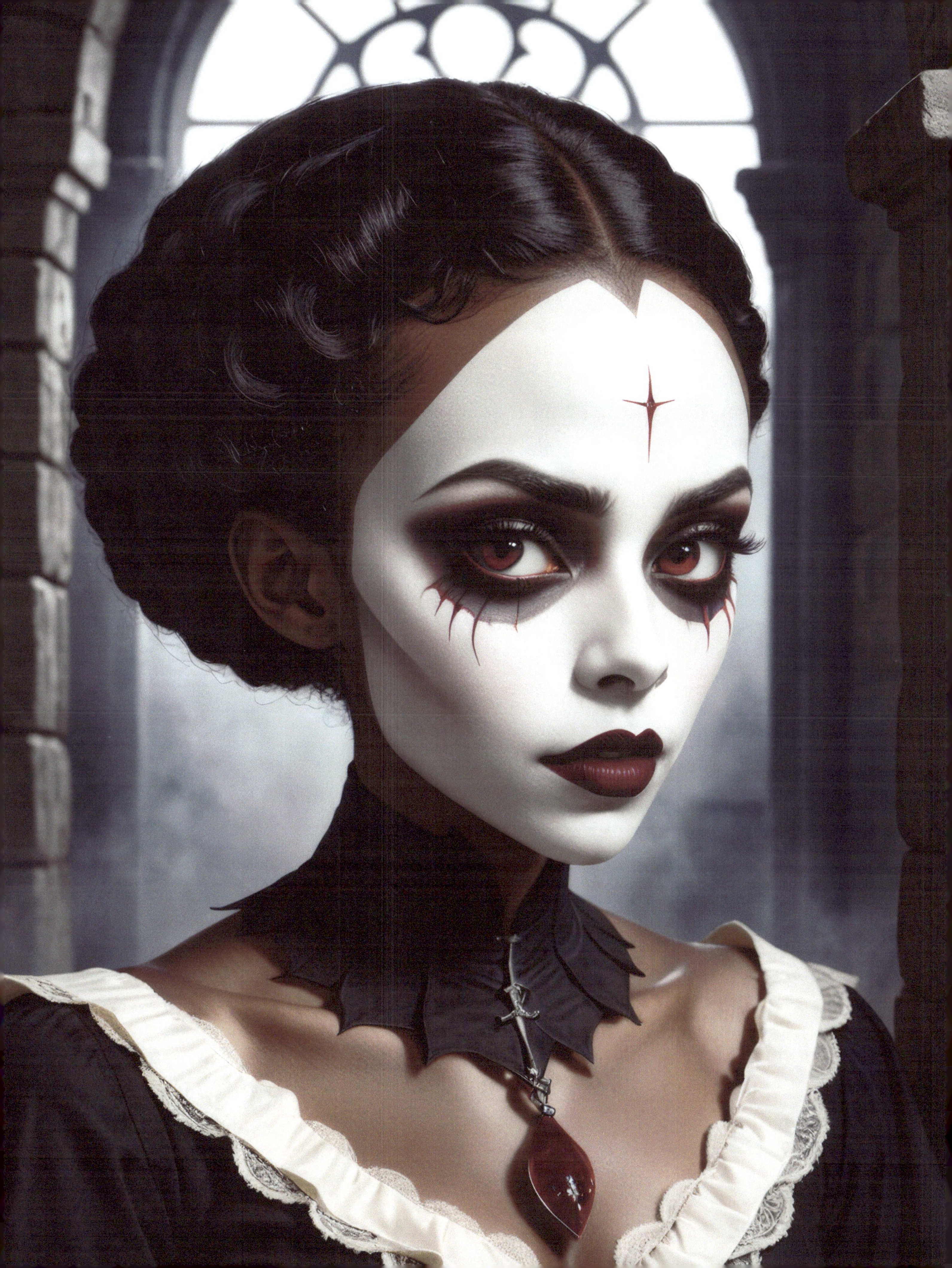

TWISTED VILLAINESS COSPLAY MAKEUP

STEP-BY-STEP INSTRUCTIONS:

SKIN PREPARATION:

START BY CLEANSING AND MOISTURIZING YOUR FACE. APPLY A PRIMER FOR SMOOTH, LONG-LASTING MAKEUP. USE A LIGHT FOUNDATION WHERE NEEDED, PARTICULARLY ON AREAS NOT COVERED BY FACE PAINT.

WHITE FACE BASE AND SKULL DETAILS:

APPLY WHITE FACE PAINT TO COVER MOST OF THE FACE, CREATING A SKELETAL OR MASK-LIKE BASE. USE BLACK AND RED FACE PAINT TO CREATE CUTS AND SCARS AROUND THE FOREHEAD AND MOUTH, EMPHASIZING A SINISTER SMILE. FOCUS ON BLENDING RED AND BLACK SHADES TO GIVE THE WOUNDS A FRESH, REALISTIC LOOK.

EYESHADOW AND SMOKEY EYES:

APPLY DARK BLACK OR DEEP PURPLE EYESHADOW AROUND THE EYES TO CREATE A DRAMATIC, SMOKEY LOOK. BLEND IT OUTWARDS FOR DEPTH. ADD DARK EYELINER ALONG THE UPPER AND LOWER LASH LINES, AND FINISH WITH VOLUMIZING MASCARA OR FALSE LASHES TO INTENSIFY THE EYES.

BLOOD AND GRINNING MOUTH EFFECT:

USE RED FACE PAINT OR SPECIAL EFFECTS MAKEUP TO CREATE A BLOODIED GRIN ALONG THE SIDES OF THE MOUTH. ADD JAGGED, STITCH-LIKE LINES FOR EXTRA HORROR EFFECT, MAKING THE SMILE APPEAR TORN OR FORCED. ADD SOME GLOSS OR FAKE BLOOD TO GIVE A WET, FRESHLY-CUT LOOK.

LIPS:

APPLY BOLD RED LIPSTICK, CAREFULLY BLENDING IT INTO THE PAINTED SMILE FOR A SEAMLESS EFFECT. ENSURE THAT THE LIPS ARE SHARPLY DEFINED, ADDING TO THE VILLAINOUS AESTHETIC.

FINAL TOUCHES:

STYLE YOUR HAIR WITH BOLD, RED WAVES OR WEAR A WIG TO MATCH THE THEME. ADD LEAFY ACCESSORIES FOR A NATURE-INSPIRED TWIST, AND COMPLETE THE LOOK WITH A GOTHIC COLLAR OR CHEST ARMOR FOR A MENACING, POWERFUL VIBE. USE A SETTING SPRAY TO KEEP THE MAKEUP IN PLACE FOR LONG-LASTING WEAR.

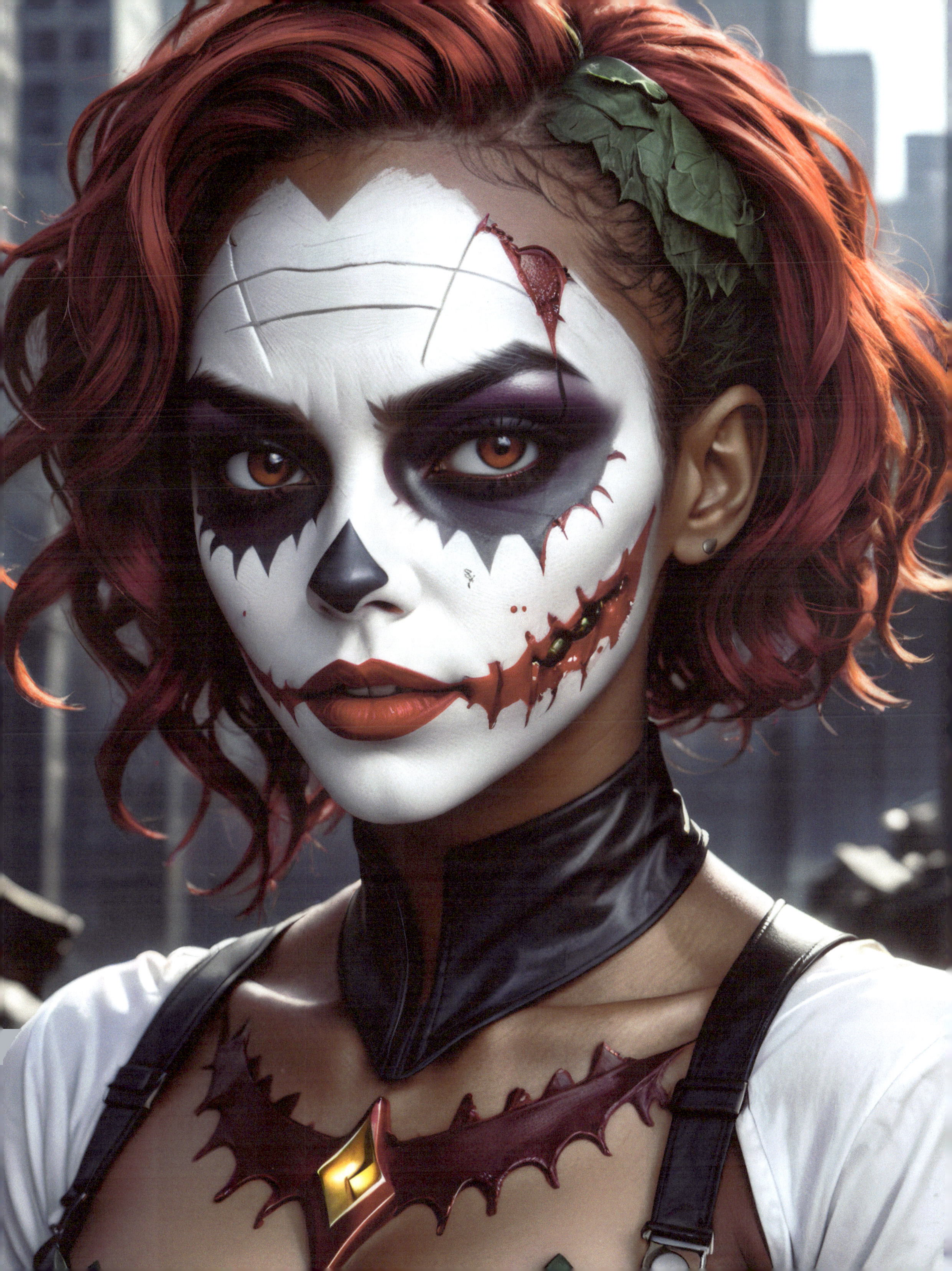

UNDEAD PIRATE CAPTAIN COSPLAY MAKEUP

STEP-BY-STEP INSTRUCTIONS:

SKIN PREPARATION:

CLEANSE AND MOISTURIZE YOUR FACE TO ENSURE SMOOTH MAKEUP APPLICATION. USE A PRIMER FOR A LONG-LASTING LOOK, FOLLOWED BY A LIGHT FOUNDATION ON AREAS NOT COVERED BY FACE PAINT.

WHITE SKULL BASE:

APPLY WHITE FACE PAINT TO COVER THE FACE, CREATING A SKELETAL STRUCTURE. FOCUS ON HOLLOWING OUT THE EYE SOCKETS WITH DARKER SHADES LIKE BLACK OR GRAY TO GIVE A SUNKEN, UNDEAD LOOK. BLEND THE EDGES AROUND THE EYES TO MAKE THE SKULL SHAPE APPEAR NATURAL.

STITCHES AND SCARS:

USE RED AND BLACK FACE PAINT TO CREATE STITCH-LIKE SCARS ALONG THE CHEEKS AND FOREHEAD. ADD THIN BLACK LINES AROUND THE MOUTH TO MIMIC A STITCHED-TOGETHER SKELETAL GRIN, AND ADD SMALL DROPS OF "BLOOD" NEAR THE STITCHES FOR EXTRA DETAIL.

DARK EYESHADOW AND CONTOUR:

APPLY BLACK OR DARK BROWN EYESHADOW AROUND THE EYES TO DEEPEN THE HOLLOWED LOOK. BLEND THE EYESHADOW OUTWARD FOR A SMOKY EFFECT, GIVING THE EYES A DRAMATIC, SUNKEN APPEARANCE. LIGHTLY CONTOUR THE CHEEKBONES AND TEMPLES WITH GRAY OR BLACK SHADES TO ENHANCE THE SKELETAL STRUCTURE.

SKULL ACCENTS:

USE A SKULL-SHAPED ACCESSORY OR FACE PROSTHETIC ON THE FOREHEAD TO ADD DEPTH AND DIMENSION TO THE LOOK. YOU CAN ALSO DRAW ADDITIONAL CRACKS OR BONE-LIKE DETAILS USING BLACK FACE PAINT FOR ADDED REALISM.

FINAL TOUCHES:

STYLE YOUR HAIR IN DREADLOCKS OR USE A PIRATE-THEMED WIG TO ENHANCE THE UNDEAD PIRATE AESTHETIC. FINISH WITH A PIRATE HAT AND WORN, RUGGED CLOTHING FOR A COMPLETE UNDEAD CAPTAIN LOOK. SET THE MAKEUP WITH A SETTING SPRAY TO ENSURE IT LASTS THROUGHOUT THE EVENT OR PERFORMANCE.

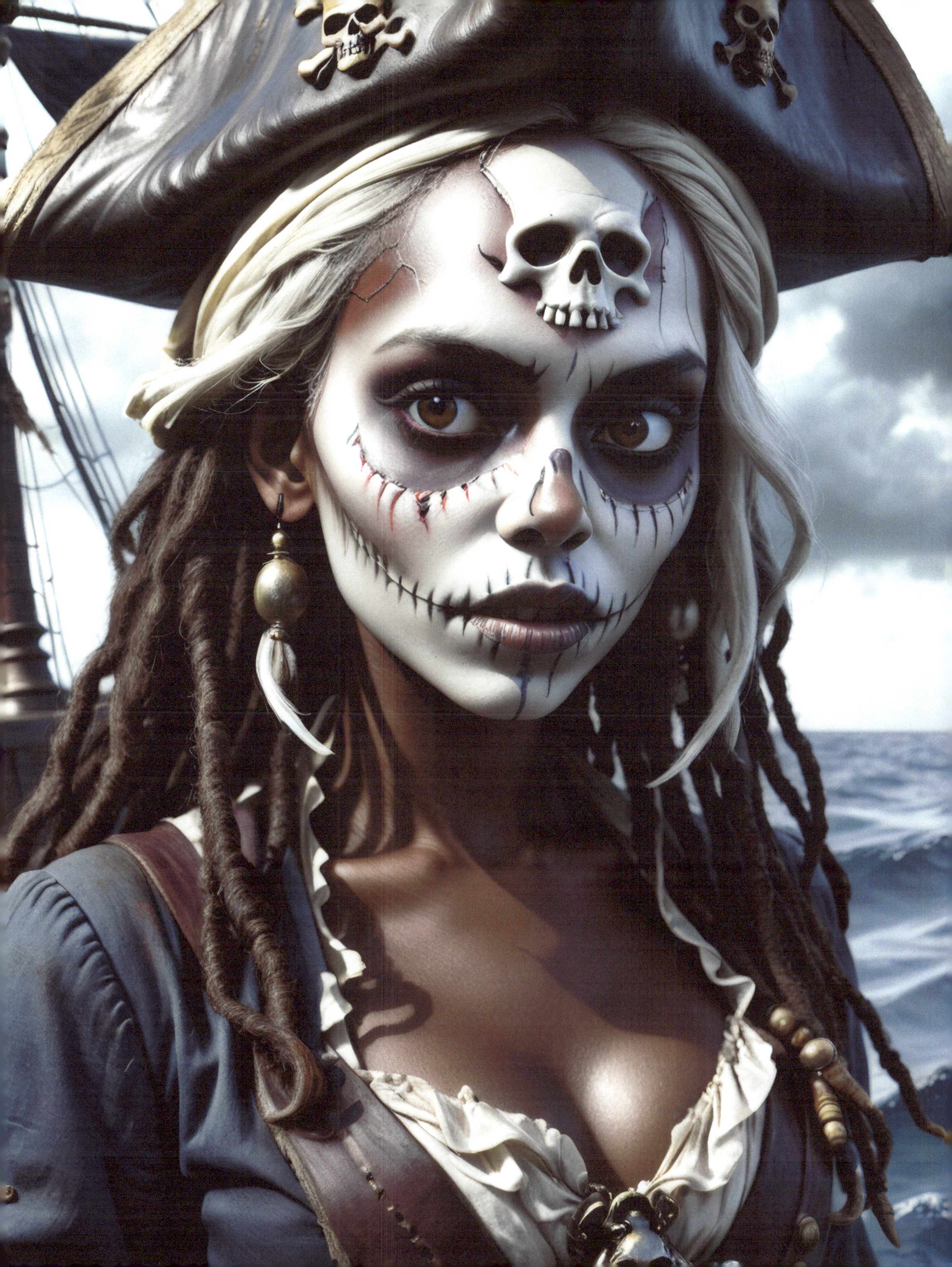

BROKEN MASKED BEAUTY COSPLAY MAKEUP

STEP-BY-STEP INSTRUCTIONS

SKIN PREPARATION:

START BY CLEANSING AND MOISTURIZING YOUR FACE TO CREATE A SMOOTH BASE. APPLY A PRIMER TO ENSURE THE MAKEUP LASTS THROUGHOUT THE DAY, FOLLOWED BY A MEDIUM-COVERAGE FOUNDATION THAT MATCHES YOUR SKIN TONE.

WHITE AND RED FACE PAINT:

APPLY WHITE FACE PAINT ON HALF OF THE FACE, FOCUSING ON CLEAN, SHARP EDGES FOR A MASK-LIKE EFFECT. ON THE EXPOSED PART OF THE FACE, USE RED FACE PAINT TO CREATE A "BROKEN" MASK EFFECT, SIMULATING CRACKED AND TORN AREAS, PARTICULARLY AROUND THE FOREHEAD AND CHEEK. ADD JAGGED EDGES AND SMALL RED DRIPS FOR A REALISTIC BLOOD-LIKE LOOK.

EYESHADOW AND EYELINER:

FOR THE EXPOSED SIDE, APPLY SOFT, NEUTRAL EYESHADOW, BLENDING A SLIGHT SMOKY EFFECT. ON THE MASKED SIDE, KEEP THE EYE MAKEUP MORE SUBTLE TO CONTRAST WITH THE DRAMATIC FACE PAINT. USE BLACK EYELINER TO LINE THE UPPER LASH LINE AND EXTEND A SMALL WING FOR DEFINITION. APPLY MASCARA OR FALSE LASHES FOR EXTRA VOLUME.

LIPS:

USE A BOLD RED LIPSTICK TO ENHANCE THE LOOK, KEEPING THE LIP SHAPE SHARP AND DEFINED. THE RED LIPS WILL COMPLEMENT THE BLOOD-LIKE DETAILS ON THE MASK, ADDING TO THE DRAMATIC EFFECT.

BROWS AND LASHES:

SHAPE AND DEFINE THE EYEBROWS USING A DARK BROW PENCIL. KEEP THE BROWS SHARP AND NATURAL, ENSURING THEY BALANCE WITH THE MAKEUP. ADD MASCARA OR FALSE LASHES FOR A FULLER, MORE INTENSE LOOK.

FINAL TOUCHES:

STYLE YOUR HAIR IN SOFT WAVES, LIKE YOUR COVER MODEL, OR LEAVE IT SLEEK TO MAINTAIN A POLISHED, FIERCE LOOK. CONSIDER PAIRING WITH GOLD ACCESSORIES, SUCH AS EARRINGS, FOR A SOPHISTICATED TOUCH. FINISH WITH A SETTING SPRAY TO ENSURE THE MAKEUP STAYS INTACT DURING ANY EVENT OR PHOTOSHOOT.

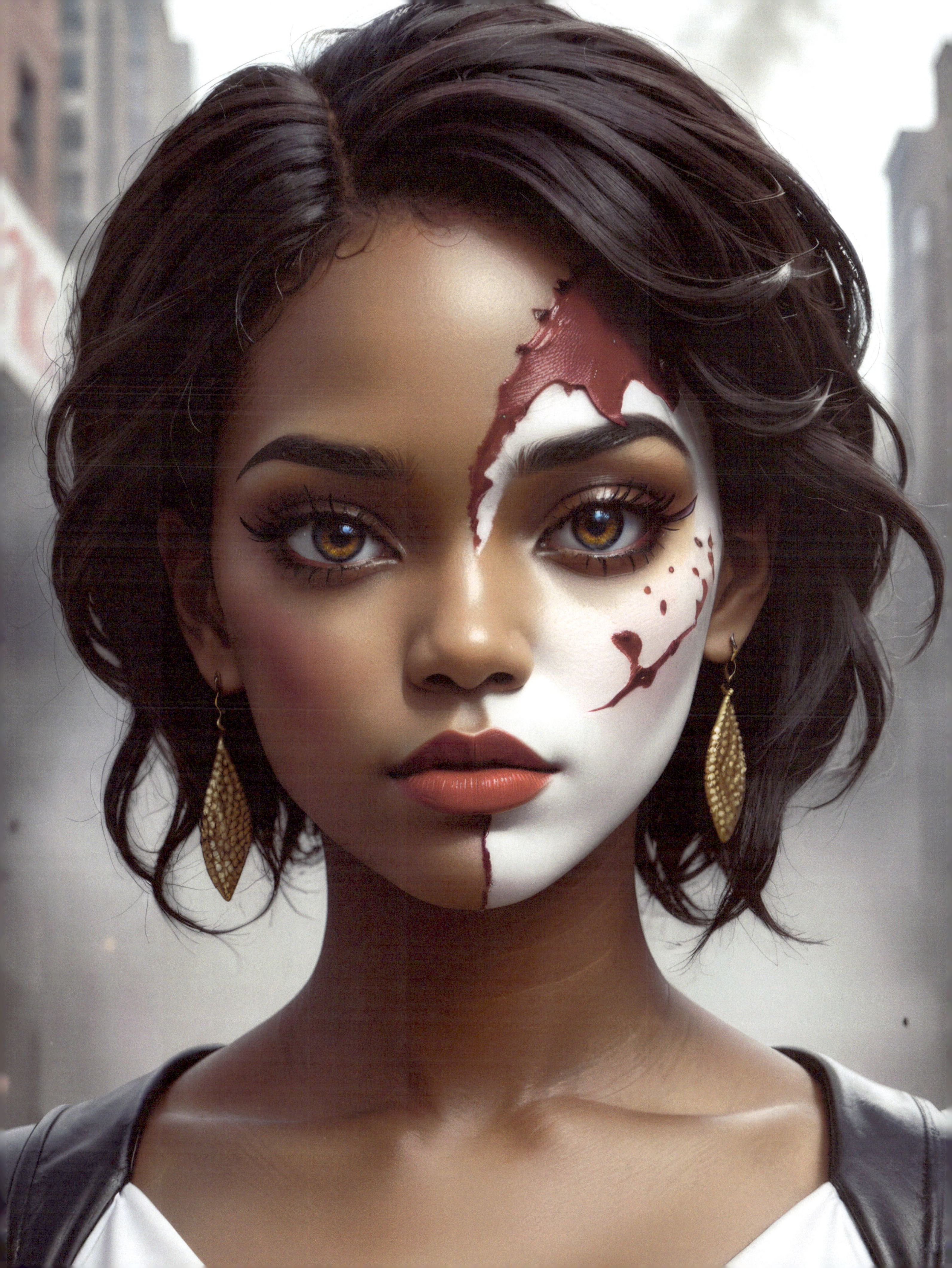

GHOSTLY TRICKSTER COSPLAY MAKEUP-COVER LOOK

STEP-BY-STEP INSTRUCTIONS:(INSPIRED BY COVER MODEL):

SKIN PREPARATION:

BEGIN BY CLEANSING AND MOISTURIZING YOUR FACE. APPLY A PRIMER FOR SMOOTH APPLICATION AND LONG-LASTING WEAR. USE A LIGHT FOUNDATION ON ANY AREAS NOT COVERED BY FACE PAINT FOR A SEAMLESS BASE.

WHITE FACE PAINT BASE:

COVER THE ENTIRE FACE WITH WHITE FACE PAINT, FOCUSING ON CREATING AN EVEN LAYER. BLEND AROUND THE HAIRLINE AND JAWLINE FOR A SMOOTH, MASK-LIKE FINISH.

PURPLE AND GREEN EYESHADOW:

APPLY DEEP PURPLE EYESHADOW AROUND THE EYES, BLENDING OUTWARD TO CREATE A SMOKEY, DRAMATIC LOOK. USE GREEN FACE PAINT OR EYESHADOW TO CREATE EXAGGERATED, STYLIZED LINES ABOVE THE EYEBROWS, MIMICKING THE CHARACTER'S WILD NATURE. BLEND THE COLORS SOFTLY FOR A COHESIVE, ARTISTIC EFFECT.

EYES AND LASHES:

USE BLACK EYELINER TO DEFINE THE UPPER AND LOWER LASH LINES, ADDING A SHARP, EXTENDED WING. APPLY VOLUMIZING MASCARA OR FALSE LASHES TO ENHANCE THE EYES, MAKING THEM STAND OUT AGAINST THE BOLD EYESHADOW.

LIPS AND CONTOUR:

USE A DEEP BURGUNDY OR PURPLE LIPSTICK TO CREATE A BOLD, DARK LIP THAT COMPLEMENTS THE EYE MAKEUP. LIGHTLY CONTOUR THE CHEEKBONES WITH A GRAY OR PURPLE HUE TO ENHANCE THE SHARP, MISCHIEVOUS LOOK OF THE MAKEUP.

FINAL TOUCHES:

STYLE YOUR HAIR IN VOLUMINOUS WAVES, ADDING VIBRANT PURPLE AND GREEN HIGHLIGHTS FOR A STRIKING, ECCENTRIC APPEARANCE. FINISH THE LOOK WITH A STRIPED OUTFIT AND GREEN BOWTIE TO COMPLETE THE TRICKSTER AESTHETIC. USE SETTING SPRAY TO KEEP THE MAKEUP IN PLACE THROUGHOUT YOUR EVENT.

CONCLUSION AND THANK YOU

THANK YOU FOR CHOOSING OUR BOOK AND EMBARKING ON THIS CREATIVE JOURNEY INTO THE WORLD OF COSPLAY MAKEUP. WE HOPE THAT OUR STEP-BY-STEP INSTRUCTIONS, INSPIRATIONS, AND TIPS HAVE EMPOWERED YOU TO CREATE STRIKING AND UNFORGETTABLE LOOKS THAT BRING YOUR CHARACTERS TO LIFE.

EACH PROJECT IN THIS BOOK WAS DESIGNED WITH YOU IN MIND — YOUR CREATIVITY, YOUR PASSION FOR COSPLAY, AND YOUR DESIRE TO EXPLORE NEW WAYS OF EXPRESSING YOURSELF. WHETHER IT'S MASTERING INTRICATE FACE PAINT TECHNIQUES OR CRAFTING BOLD, DRAMATIC LOOKS, WE HOPE THIS BOOK HAS INSPIRED YOU TO PUSH THE BOUNDARIES OF YOUR ARTISTRY.

REMEMBER, MAKEUP IS A LIMITLESS FORM OF SELF-EXPRESSION. EVERY BRUSHSTROKE AND EVERY COLOR CHOICE IS A CHANCE TO CREATE SOMETHING PERSONAL AND UNIQUE. LET THIS BOOK CONTINUE TO INSPIRE YOU FOR YEARS TO COME, ENCOURAGING YOU TO EXPERIMENT, INNOVATE, AND DISCOVER NEW TECHNIQUES THAT WILL HELP YOU GROW AS AN ARTIST.

ONCE AGAIN, THANK YOU FOR CHOOSING OUR BOOK. YOUR SUPPORT ALLOWS US TO CONTINUE CREATING MATERIALS THAT FUEL YOUR CREATIVITY AND PASSION FOR MAKEUP. WE WISH YOU MANY JOYFUL, INVENTIVE MOMENTS WITH YOUR COSPLAY LOOKS, AND COUNTLESS EXCITING TRANSFORMATIONS AHEAD!